DISCARD

AUG 1995

Cross-Cultural Marriages and the Church

Also by J. Lawrence Driskill

Mission Adventures in Many Lands

Japan Diary of Cross-Cultural Mission

Mission Stories from Around the World

Cross-Cultural Marriages and the Church

Living the Global Neighborhood

J. Lawrence Driskill

Hope Publishing House
Pasadena, California

Copyright © 1995 J. Lawrence Driskill

All rights reserved.

For information address:
Hope Publishing House
Southern California Ecumenical Council
P.O. Box 60008
Pasadena, CA 91116 - U.S.A.
Tel: (818) 792-6123 / Fax: (818) 792-2121

Cover design — Michael McClary/The Workshop

Cover photo — Gerson & Elisa Ribeiro with Kelly, Paulo and Marieli

Printed in the U.S.A. on acid-free paper

Library of Congress Cataloging-in-Publication Data

Driskill, J. Lawrence, 1920-
　　Cross-cultural marriages and the church : living the global neighborhood / by J. Lawrence Driskill.
　　　　p.　　cm.
　　Includes bibliographical references (p.　).
　　ISBN 0-932727-81-6 (alk. paper) : $15.95. -- ISBN 0-932727-80-8 (pbk. : alk. paper) : $9.95
　　1. Marriage--Religious aspects--Christianity. 2. Interracial marriage--Case studies. 3. Intermarriage--Case studies. I. Title.
BV835.D75　1995
248.8'44--dc20　　　　　　　　　　　　　　　　　　　94-41144
　　　　　　　　　　　　　　　　　　　　　　　　　　　　CIP

Gratefully dedicated
to those whose stories
appear in this book.

Acknowledgements

First I want to thank those whose interracial and intercultural stories appear in this book. They are the ones who provided most of the information needed for this study. For special reasons, the names of those people whose stories are told in chapters 5, 8, 12 and 14 have been changed to protect their anonymity.

I also need to thank Ms. Osanna Love Gooding and the Westminster Gardens Writers' Group for their comments and suggestions. When that group was in recess, Ms. Mildred Brown helped me with her evaluation of some of the stories.

Dr. J. Christy Wilson, Jr. kindly wrote the foreword and gave me many good suggestions.

Four Christian leaders provided helpful commendations, recommending the book to prospective readers: Dr. Fred Prinzing, Dr. Clifton Kirkpatrick, Professor George Larsen and Dr. Gordon Kirk.

And I am most grateful to my editor and publisher, Faith Annette Sand, and her assistant, Susan Parry, for helping to prepare the book for publication.

Contents

	Foreword, *Dr. J. Christy Wilson* viii
	Introduction ix
1.	Biblical Insights on Cross-Cultural Marriages 1
2.	Across Class Lines in Japan 7
3.	A Will to Succeed 13
4.	An American Mixed Marriage 20
5.	The Foolish Rush* 25
6.	A Chinese-Japanese Love Story 31
7.	A Thai-Filipino Shared Ministry 37
8.	Irreconcilable Differences* 45
9.	Witnessing Together in Korea 51
10.	Happiness Is Where You Find It 59
11.	Bridging Traditional Animosities 64
12.	Unraveling Ties That Bind* 69
13.	A Japanese-Latino Partnership 73
14.	A Rejected Korean War Bride* 77
15.	Expanding Horizons 81
16.	A Three-Culture Life 87
17.	The Best of Japan and America 93
18.	Overcoming Intercultural Barriers 97
19.	Conclusion 105
	Interracial Organizations 109
	Bibliography for Further Study 113

* Names have been changed to protect anonymity.

Foreword

With the greater mixing of nationalities and races today more than ever before, author J. Lawrence Driskill observes there are increasingly more international and interracial marriages. How are we to view these?

From actual case studies of couples coming from different nations and races, he gives valuable insights, demonstrating the dangers and illustrating the secrets of success for such marriages. Couples, their families and friends can get many helpful hints from these stories from real life.

In these days of high divorce rates among those of the same race and nationality, it is useful to have a book which deals with a further dimension of difficulty. The Prophet Amos in the eighth century B.C. asked the question, "Can two walk together except they be agreed?" The author here shows that the strongest bond in international and interracial marriages is a mutually shared faith in Jesus Christ as Lord and Savior. When difficulties arise, as they will, such couples are able to apologize to one another and seek forgiveness from each other and also from their God.

This is the reason the Bible warns Christians not to be unequally yoked together with unbelievers. Paul in 1 Corinthians 7:30 writes that Christian widows are free to marry again, but they must only marry a husband who knows the Lord.

God who has created everyone has neither racial nor national prejudice. God will have people from all languages, tribes, races and nations in heaven (Rev 5:9 and 7:9). We then as believers will all be the Bride of Christ and thus participators in the greatest international and interracial marriage in history—which will last throughout eternity.

—*J. Christy Wilson, Jr.*
Emeritus Professor, World Evangelization, Gordon-Conwell Seminary

Introduction

As international trade, travel, student exchanges and other international contacts have increased, so have cross-cultural marriages. The rate is highest among military personnel serving in other countries and in students studying abroad. Regrettably, in their romantic idealism and immaturity, some of these young people enter interracial marriages without fully considering the problems that can develop—often with unhappy results.

After retiring from missionary service to Japan, I began to serve part-time in a Japanese-American church in Altadena, California where it is my responsibility to befriend and counsel the 15 interracial couples related to that church. This book arose out of that experience after an Afro-American married to a woman from Japan asked that I share some of the insights derived from assisting various cross-cultural couples learn to understand and communicate with each other. This particular couple, realizing they needed help, had come to our church. When others heard about the project, they agreed to share their interracial marriage stories in an effort to aid one another.

Another impetus for this study came from hearing author Marianne Alireza tell of her marriage to a Muslim from Saudia Arabia. Speaking at our church, this American Christian told how in that country she was seldom allowed to go out in public and when she did, she had to wear a veil over her face. Cultural restrictions kept her from attending mixed parties, public movies, restaurants or even from strolling the streets, let alone the stores. Her life revolved almost wholly around the home with her extended family. She raised five children in this atmosphere only to have her Muslim husband divorce her in order to marry another woman.

Listening to her story, I was amazed she showed no bitterness toward her ex-husband, even though he rejected her. But she did open my eyes to how difficult an interracial marriage can become when both culture and religion are different.

In my study I had expected the divorce rate to be higher among interracial couples than in the general population—and with military personnel that seems to be true. However, I was surprised to find that in the marriages I studied this was not the case. It would seem that in the marriages I came to know best within the church there were limited failures. How to account for this success rate? Apparently the mitigating factors here are that many of these couples were fairly mature when they married—and since they were within the church community they had a common faith and similar values. Obviously they also were making an effort to appreciate each other's culture.

Anecdotal evidence would indicate that interracial marriages which are also religiously mixed marriages are more problematic than those where a common faith is shared across ethnic or racial boundaries. This would indicate that religion is a more important factor than race in such marriages.

Up until a few years ago race was broadly defined under three categories of skin color: blacks, whites and yellows. *Webster's* now defines "race" more specifically, as including "a family, tribe, people, or nation belonging to the same stock."

Even this may be too broad for we now know that the Japanese are a "mixed" race including Caucasoid Ainu "stock" with non-Oriental characteristics such as blue eyes and much body hair and even some Polynesian strain present. Thus it is hard for any to claim to be a "pure" race as most nations are increasingly becoming racially mixed.

This book records case studies of interracial marriages involving people from 13 different countries or races. Most of the stories provide good role models, demonstrating how to make an interracial marriage succeed. Several stories describe how some cross-cultural marriages fail—highlighting problems that need to be overcome and pitfalls to be avoided if a marriage is to work.

Of the 17 marriages presented here, twelve were interracial, international and intercultural. Four were interracial but not international. One was international and intercultural but not interracial, but was included to show how severe culture shock can affect a marriage. Some might feel that marriages between Japanese, Chinese and Koreans should not be considered "interracial" since they are all "Orientals." However, since they themselves seem to regard themselves as separate races, we conceded to this nomenclature.

As to overcoming problems and prejudices, I learned much from Fred and Anita Prinzing, Caucasian parents who wrote *Mixed Messages: Responding to Interracial Marriage* about two of their children who married Afro-Americans. Their discussion of suppressed prejudices and the testing of their Christian value system, emphasizes the importance of Christian love if we are to find the glue that finally binds all relationships together.

Since it is obvious that interracial marriages are increasing—in our society and our churches—then as Christians we must face this issue responsibly so we are prepared to help solve problems that may arise.

1

Biblical Insights on Cross-Cultural Marriages

Interracial or cross-cultural marriages are found early in the Biblical record. When Abraham's wife, Sarah, was unable to produce children, she gave her Egyptian maid, Hagar, to Abraham to bear children for her. While technically a concubine, Hagar did provide Abraham with a son, Ishmael, and so fulfilled a relationship and function usually associated with a wife (Gen 16:41ff). Hagar later chose an Egyptian wife for Abraham's son, Ishmael (Gen 21:21).

Present-day Jews trace their ancestry back to Abraham because Sarah did finally produce a son, Isaac, for Abraham. Many Arabs today also trace their ancestry back to Abraham through his son, Ishmael. Since racial lines were not clearly separated in Old Testament marriages, it may be better to refer to mixed marriages as international, or interethnic, rather than interracial at that time.

Esau, one of Isaac's sons, "took his wives from the women of Canaan." These included Adah, a Hittite woman; Cholibamah, a Hivite woman; and Basemath, who some scholars think was also a Hittite (Gen 36:2-3).

Jacob's son, Joseph, sold into slavery in Egypt by his jealous brothers, became a valued leader in Pharaoh's court. Pharaoh gave Joseph an Egyptian wife, Asenath, who was the daughter of a priest of On—or Heliopolis (Gen 41:45ff). Two sons of Joseph and Asenath, Manasseh and Ephraim, became heads of major tribes in Israel and as two of the recognized progenitors of the "twelve tribes" of Israel, there apparently was never any stigma attached to the fact that their mother was an Egyptian.

Even the great leader Moses began his married life with a foreign wife—Zipporah, daughter of Jethro, a priest of Midian (Ex 2:21ff). Later Moses married a Cushite (Ethiopian) wife and was severely criticized by his brother, Aaron, and his sister, Miriam (Num 12:1ff). God then rebukes Aaron and Miriam for criticizing the "humble" Moses and Miriam is stricken with leprosy because she dared to oppose God's chosen servant. When Moses appeals to God, Miriam is healed.

According to the book of Judges (3:6ff), it was a common practice for Hebrews to intermarry with foreigners. "The Israelites lived among the Canaanites, Hittites, Amorites, Perizzites, Hivites and Jebusites. They took their daughters in marriage and gave their own daughters to their sons, and served their gods." Of course, the statement, "and served their gods," indicates a serious problem that developed in Israel—idolatry and worshipping "other" gods.

Throughout Scriptures there are many references to the danger of being corrupted by foreign gods. Most of these make it clear that the defilement comes not because of the race or nationality of the foreign spouses but from their idolatrous religious practice—a factor which impacts cross-cultural marriages today. Thus Deuteronomy warns, "Do not intermarry with them...for they will turn your children away from following me to serve other gods" (7:3-4). (See also Gen 24:3 and 28:1 as well as Josh 23:12-13).

One of the greatest love stories in history developed from the cross-cultural marriages of Naomi's sons, Mahlon and Kilion, to Moabite women. Ruth, one of the Moabite women, chooses to follow Naomi back to Israel after Ruth's husband dies. Naomi, having buried her husband as well as her two sons in Moab, wants to return to Israel but she doesn't want to force her widowed daughters-in-law to go with her.

Ruth refuses to be abandoned and says to Naomi, "Don't urge me to leave you or to turn back from you. Where you go I will go, and where you stay I will stay. Your people will be my people and your God my God. Where you die I will die, and there I will be buried. May the Lord deal with me, be it ever so severely, if anything but death separates you and me." (Ruth 1:4, 16-18).

Her devotion to Naomi results in an oft-recited love story. At Naomi's urging Ruth develops a relationship with Boaz, an Israelite relative of Naomi's. The cross-cultural marriage that results also crosses social class lines for Boaz is a rich man, whereas the two women were so poor Ruth had to stoop to charity—by gleaning what was left in Boaz's grain fields after his reapers had done their work.

A most significant issue from this international marriage was our Lord Jesus Christ, a direct descendent of that marriage. Ruth and Boaz gave birth to Obed, the father of Jesse, the father of King David, from whom Jesus Christ was descended (Ruth 4:13-17; Mt 1:1 and 9:27). An interesting antecedent to this lineage was Rahab, the harlot of Jericho, who married Salmon and bore Boaz, making Rahab another cross-cultural ancestor of Jesus Christ (Mt 1:5).

Throughout Scriptures many international marriages are noted. David "took more concubines and wives in Jerusalem" (2 Sam 5:13) including Bathsheba, wife of Uriah the Hittite. Whether she was a Hittite or not is uncertain, but she could have been one of David's foreign wives (2 Sam 11:26-12:24). This marriage came about through lust and subtly contrived murder—terrible sins that David laments and repents of in Psalm 51. Yet this tragic marriage produced Solomon, Israel's third king who became the richest and wisest king in all of Israel's history.

Solomon married many foreign wives. It is recorded that "He had 700 wives of royal birth and 300 concubines, and his wives led him astray. As Solomon grew old, his wives turned his heart after other gods, and his heart was not fully devoted to the Lord his God, as the heart of David his father had been. He followed Ashtoreth the goddess of the Sidonians, and Molech the detestable god of the Ammonites" (1 Kings 11:3-5). Solomon was corrupted, but we must be careful to note that it was not the problem of race or nationality, but the issue of false religions—a distinction we must make throughout our Biblical study.

Rehoboam, Solomon's son, was born out of the cross-cultural marriage of Solomon to Naamah, an Ammonite woman. He became the fourth king of Israel and had 18 wives and 60 concubines and knowing the international marriage record of his father, we can assume that some of Rehoboam's marriages were international (2 Chr 11:18-23). (See also Ezra 9 & 10 and

Neh 13:23-30 on other marriages.)

In the first three years of his reign Rehoboam was said to be faithful to Yahweh. Apparently the following year he allowed the Ammonite gods of his mother to gain some recognition in Israel. After a disastrous defeat by the Egyptian Pharaoh, Shishak, Rehoboam repented and again, at least to some degree, became faithful to Yahweh (2 Chr 12:1ff).

By the time the New Testament was written, international trade and travel had become so common, along with cross-cultural marriages, that such marriages no longer seemed to attract the attention given them in the Old Testament. However, it is in the New Testament that we find a good theological basis for international and interracial marriages. In speaking to the people at Athens, Paul points out the basic unity among all humanity. "The God who made the world and everything in it, he who is Lord of heaven and earth ... From one ancestor he made all nations to inhabit the whole earth, and he allotted the times of their existence and the boundaries of the places where they would live ... For 'In him we live and move and have our being'; as even some of your own poets have said, 'For we too are his offspring' " (Acts 17:24-28).

The King James version translates this, "hath made of one blood all nations" (v. 26). While "one blood" may not be a literal translation of the Greek original, it does assert an essential truth. Medical science tells us that all races have the same basic blood types. Since God created all races, it is wrong for us to say that any one race is "superior" or "inferior" to another. They are all equal in God's sight, and we should not try to deny that basic equality by making judgmental statements.

But we do know that a cross-cultural or interracial marriage is much more likely to succeed if both husband and wife are united by a common faith in Jesus Christ. Paul says that "in Christ" we are all one: "There is neither Jew nor Greek (race doesn't matter), slave nor free (social class doesn't matter), male nor female (gender differences don't matter), for you are all one in Christ Jesus" (Gal 3:28).

The danger in mixed marriages lies not in problems of race or nationality, but in being yoked with those who do not believe in God's revelation in Jesus Christ. "Do not be yoked together with unbelievers....What harmony is there between Christ and Belial?" (2 Cor 6:14-18; see also Deut 22:10). Imperative in an interracial marriage, as in any marriage, is a common relationship to Jesus Christ. If both spouses have a primary loyalty to Christ they will have a better understanding of the love, patience, forgiveness and coöperative spirit needed to make their marriage succeed. Having the "fruit of the Spirit" is an asset to any marriage: "The fruit of the Spirit is love, joy, peace, patience, kindness, goodness, faithfulness, gentleness and self-control" (Gal 5:22).

Our military establishment brings young people together cross-culturally when members of the armed forces are sent to serve their duty in another country. Also students studying in a foreign country meet and fall in love across national borders. In their romantic idealism many such couples overlook the hardships they face in these marriages. As Christians we must share with them the Biblical basis for interracial marriage and the church must help them receive the "fruit of the Spirit" needed to make their marriages succeed.

2

Across Class Lines in Japan

My first close contact with an interracial marriage happened during my early years as a missionary in Japan. The architect for our new missionary home proved to be Merrell Vories, a long-term American missionary to Japan who had married a Japanese woman and become a Japanese citizen. His wife, Maki Hitotsuyanagi, was related to the emperor's family, so Merrell had married a member of the Japanese nobility.

Merrell appeared at first to be a perpetual bachelor. After having served in Japan for a dozen years, a close friend asked,

"Why have you never married? You could certainly use a good wife to help in your mission work."

"Well, there are two reasons," replied Merrell. "First, I have never met a woman I felt I wanted to spend the rest of my life with and second, I am not sure any woman would want to share the long hours and hard work of my mission work. Few women would want to endure the sacrifices necessary to share in my mission dreams, and struggle to realize those dreams. Maybe my work requires that I give up thoughts of marriage. After all, I am already in my late thirties, pretty late to find a suitable partner."

Merrell didn't know it but his future wife, Maki, was also doubting she would ever find a suitable husband. Several times her father had arranged an *omiai* (marriage partner introduction) for Maki but each time she decided the man was not right for her. Maki's father, a *daimyo* (feudal lord) who was related to the emperor's family, was concerned Maki should marry a man with the "right connections."

"It looks like you may become the 'old maid' of our family," scolded her father. "What can we do to prepare you for a proper marriage? How about sending you to America for a couple of years to study? Maybe that would help prepare you for a good marriage."

"I like the idea," replied Maki. "I have always wanted to study in America and see what new things I can learn there."

After her agreed-upon years of study, Maki wrote home, "I want to stay longer. I like this place and want to learn more."

"No, you must come home now," answered her father and mother. "Maybe we can arrange a good marriage for you—before it is too late. We will no longer send money for you to stay in America. Come home right away!"

"You don't need to send money to support me in America," answered Maki. "I have a job here and can support myself."

This was shocking news to her family. No member of the nobility was supposed to lower themselves by doing "lucrative labor." But Maki was a strong-willed woman and stayed in America for nine years. During this time she not only became even more of a "liberated soul" but she also became a Christian. In all her family there was only one other Christian, Madame Asako Hirooka, a nationally known woman with great influence. Thus Maki was not completely without a Christian supporter in her extended family.

Maki learned many things in America, including what good American homes were like. Back in Japan, she was asked to be an adviser to her brother in the building of a fine new home he was planning. The architect for that home was Merrell Vories, who as a trained architect had started an architectural firm to support his mission work.

When Merrell first came to Japan, he worked under the auspices of the YMCA as an English teacher in a public school. He was forbidden to verbalize his Christian witness in the classroom, but he won many students to Christ by having them come to his home in the evenings or on holidays for Bible studies. This made him unpopular among certain leaders in the community and he was fired. Apologizing for letting him go, the principal of the public school said, "We knew you would be teaching about Jesus in your home, but we didn't think anyone would believe you. Too many students are becoming Christians. We must fire you."

After teaching private students for awhile, Merrell got what turned into a thriving architectural business going where he eventually met Maki. At first as they worked together on the new house plans no romantic sparks flew between Merrell and Maki, but they did find they shared many common dreams and values. They had similar ideas regarding individual character development and for developing an ideal society. Eventually they grew so close that Merrell said, "Maki, I have grown to love you. Will you marry me?"

"Yes," answered Maki, "but it may take some time to get my family to agree to it. This is something new and strange for them."

The family's opposition was fierce. Her father said, "For over 2,000 years no person of the nobility has ever forsaken their royal name and national heritage to marry a foreigner. You are making a great mistake!"

It took over a year of delicate negotiations with Maki's family and the leaders of the imperial household, but finally with the strong support of Maki's Christian relative, Madame Asako Hirooka, approval was given. The family gave them a sumptuous wedding in Tokyo—and this unusual wedding created quite a stir in this capital city of Japan.

The wedding was held in the chapel of Meiji Gakuin College, which Merrell's architectural firm had designed. The reception was held in Maki's brother's home, which had served as the "matchmaker" to bring them together. They honeymooned in a cottage Merrell had designed and owned at the famous resort of Karuizawa. As Merrell said, "No architect could ask for a happier setting for the greatest event of his life."

By this time Merrell's "Omi Brotherhood Mission" was flourishing with many churches, schools and even a mentholatum factory with the income from the factory providing a major source of support for the mission work. Merrell was convinced his bride would help the Mission grow even more.

When they first were married, Merrell's Christian co-workers were skeptical about the relationship succeeding. They said, "How can this 'princess' ever become one of us? She has never done housework, so how can she learn to cook, clean house and do the 'grubby tasks' that normally come our way?"

To their amazement and joy Maki soon learned to outdo most of them in all kinds of chores. But her specialty was in education. With great zeal she helped to advance the mission's schools and churches.

When Merrell was asked why their interracial marriage turned out so well, he replied, "Many things contributed, I'm sure. We both had some previous knowledge of each other's language and culture; we shared a common religion and philosophy of life; we have mutual interests in work and recreation and we each got to know the other's family and friends quite well. But the most important thing is that we both love God and God's people, as well as one another. And we know that Christian love includes Christian forgiveness—essential to any good marriage."

I asked Merrell, "Just how much of a problem is the racial difference in mixed marriages?"

"My conviction," replied Merrell, "is that racial differences are less of a problem than other things—such as personality differences, religious disagreements, disparity in value systems and expectations—which seem to me much harder to overcome than cross-cultural or racial dissimilarities. In other words, compatibility of character, religion, values and common interests are more important than race."

Of course Merrell and Maki's relationship is unique in

several ways. Theirs was the first marriage the Japanese nobility officially approved between a family member and a Caucasian. This was the first time anyone from the ranks of Japanese nobility voluntarily "humbled" herself and became like a "servant" to those around her, following the example of her Lord Jesus Christ (Phil 2:7-8). Although from a higher social class, Maki chose to become "equal" in service and mutual support with the Christians and non-Christians around her. This also appears to be the first time an American missionary became a Japanese citizen—in a conscious effort to enhance his mission work and his interracial marriage.

So this marriage across social lines was nurtured by their mutual commitment and dedication to Christ. Having learned from Jesus the meaning of Christian love, forgiveness and mutual support, they were able to overcome the problems they encountered along their pilgrimage. Surely this is a good place to start whenever anyone in the church community seeks to counsel with, and help, interracial couples today.

3

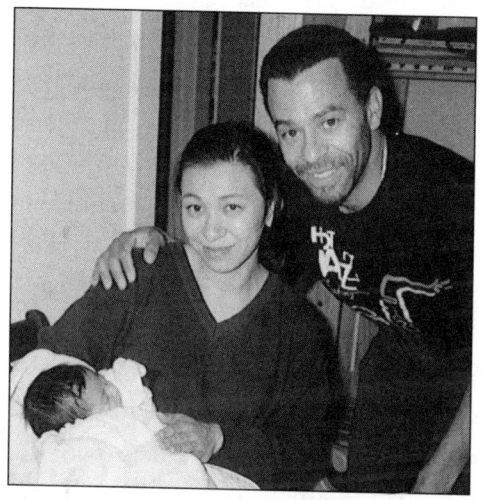

A Will to Succeed

Kenny Elliott is a professional musician who travels all over the world as a drummer with the band of the famous singer, Lou Rawls. In April 1989 Kenny went on a musical tour to Tokyo, Japan and after performing with a Japanese organist from Osaka, Toshihiko Kankawa, he decided to visit a Tokyo nightclub to check out the local music scene.

There Kenny met an attractive young Japanese woman named Sumika who was there with friends. They began conversing about music—using her limited English plus some translation help from a friend. Sumika, who majored in music in school, admitted that she both sang and played the piano.

Before long Kenny asked whether she would like to come to hear their musical performance the next evening.

With a shy smile, Sumika turned to her friend and said, "Shall we go to hear his music group tomorrow?" The friend agreed and this turned out to be the beginning of a romance between Kenny and Sumika.

With Kenny's dark brown skin and curly hair and Sumika's light brown skin and straight black hair, they made a handsome couple. Their courtship continued for two years and they got married at the Los Angeles County Court House in 1991.

I met Kenny and Sumika when they visited the Japanese-American church in Altadena, California where I often assist. As a retired missionary to Japan, I help with the translation program for a small group of people who still need to hear the sermon in Japanese. I also conduct a monthly fellowship and Bible study meeting in Japanese.

Kenny learned about the Japanese-American church from a member, Ron Ota who owns a music store Kenny frequently visits. In God's mysterious way, Kenny and Sumika were led to buy a home only two blocks away from the church and Kenny felt that attending this church might help Sumika feel more at home in this strange new land of America.

Kenny was raised in an Afro-American family who were active Christians and he felt the need of God's help in making their interracial marriage succeed. Kenny's own faith had been tried and strengthened once on a flight to Oakland, California for a recording appointment. The plane passed through a violent storm and it appeared on the verge of crashing at any moment.

As the danger mounted, Kenny saw some passengers lose their nerve and begin to scream. After some immediate fear, Kenny prayed for the Lord to take him to heaven if he must die. Then, Kenny felt strangely calm, thinking, "God is with me. Whatever happens I know I am in God's loving care."

Now Kenny was facing another kind of storm—the communication problems and misunderstandings in his interracial marriage made him realize he again felt a great need for God's help. It meant sitting through some meetings in Japanese, which he couldn't understand, but Kenny was a faithful attender. He was willing to do whatever he could to help his Japanese wife get acclimated to a strange land and find some Japanese friends who would help her. Kenny also admitted that they soon realized they needed God's intervention in their marriage if it was going to last.

After coming to church a few times, Kenny said to me, "Sumika believes in God but she needs to know more about Christianity before she can become a committed Christian. I hope that worshipping in Japanese will help Sumika come to know God's love and comfort in her own life."

Since our small Japanese-speaking group needed someone to play the piano when we sang hymns in Japanese, I asked Sumika to play for us. With her shy smile she said, "I'm not sure I can do it well. I am not accustomed to playing hymns. But if you will give me a hymnbook and let me practice I will try it." She proved to be an excellent pianist, and continues to play for us whenever she can.

As I got to know them better I asked, 'How are you getting along in your interracial marriage? Does the difference in language and culture still make it difficult to communicate?"

"Yes," answered Sumika in Japanese. "I am studying English but I don't really understand it very well, and Kenny knows only a few words in Japanese so it is hard for us to discuss problems freely."

Kenny added, "Not knowing each other's culture very well, we seem to have different views and ideals. For instance Sumika follows the Japanese tradition of being very lenient with our son, Kei, while I try to follow my family's custom of teaching discipline while the child is still small. Our ideas about child-raising just seem to be different.

"Not only that, but being 14 years older than Sumika creates an 'age gap' between us. Beyond this, I tend to be more of an analytical person than Sumika is and she seems to be more of a feeling person than I am, so we have some personality differences which make it difficult for us to discuss our problems calmly and come to some mutually agreeable solution. It is especially hard to decide how to spend our limited income in the best way possible and avoid serious financial problems. I need Sumika's help."

In Japanese Sumika said, "I had heard that American men, unlike most Japanese men, helped their wives with the housework. But Kenny doesn't help me with housework—at least not as much as I want him to. Not knowing much English, not having many friends here, and with Kenny often away on musical tours, I find life hard and frustrating here."

"What is the greatest problem you face in your marriage?" I asked.

"Our biggest hurdle," answered Kenny, "is that Sumika's family is opposed to our marriage. They seem to resent her marrying a Black man. Even though my family has welcomed

Sumika into our circle, Sumika's parents have never fully accepted me. In fact, I haven't even met them yet.

"When I wrote her parents asking why they opposed the marriage, they replied, 'To tell the truth we live in a conservative small town and we are afraid of what our friends and neighbors will think when they learn that our daughter has married a Black man. We own a small store and are afraid our customers won't buy from us anymore if you should come visit. We would be willing to meet you in a neutral place like Tokyo, but not here in our village.'

"With that attitude," added Kenny, "I became angry and hurt by their racial discrimination. I don't think I should visit them until they are ready to welcome me into their own home."

I asked Kenny, "Did your family agree to the marriage from the beginning?"

"Oh yes," answered Kenny with a laugh. "They were very happy about it. Since I was in my late thirties then, they were afraid I would never marry. It was good news to them, and they liked Sumika from the beginning."

In Japanese Sumika added, "Our son, Kei, was born in Japan. He spent the first few months of his life in my parents' home. Also I have taken him to visit his grandparents in Japan several times. They love him as their cute little grandson. Hopefully someday they will also love and welcome Kenny into our family."

When I asked Kenny what benefits he sees in an interracial marriage, he replied, "One advantage is that the children have a richer cultural background. They get to know and appreciate both cultures. I think that is also true for the husband and the wife."

"What are the disadvantages you perceive?" I asked.

Kenny answered, "I think that if couples have their goals and priorities worked out together, there may not be any disadvantages. But if they can't focus on the same values and ideals then many problems arise. They may find it difficult even to discuss some issues. Without common values, communication becomes a major problem. Also, mutual trust is very important in any marriage. If the couple can discuss things freely, minor problems won't lead to major confrontations.

"In our case, I fear the negative attitude of Sumika's parents has a negative effect on Sumika. They seem to want her to come home every time we face a problem. This makes Sumika feel torn apart by her conflicting loyalties to me and to her family and makes life hard for both of us."

"How are you trying to overcome these issues?" I asked.

"Well," replied Kenny. "We really do love each other—and we both want our marriage to succeed. With our will to succeed, I hope we can do so. The most important thing is that we are depending upon God to help us in our marriage. Thankfully, our professional counselor is a Christian."

How can we evaluate this interracial marriage? It seems that in their romantic idealism, Kenny and Sumika did not fully realize the problems that differences in language and culture could create. They also may have underestimated the difficulties a 14-year age gap plus their personality differences could cause. It might have been easier had they waited to have children until they had first adjusted more fully to each other. As it was, their first son, Kei, was born less than a year after they married.

One continuing obstacle that seems to be dissipating is the negative attitude of Sumika's parents. Although they have yet to invite him to visit, they are beginning to send valuable gifts to Kenny and seem to be learning to appreciate what a fine person he is. They recognize his many talents and also know he is gracious and forgiving enough not to let their opposition turn him against them. They are certainly proud of their two fine grandsons.

Kenny is convinced they are good people who eventually will be able to overcome their prejudice and fear of what their neighbors think about the marriage and they will eventually accept him.

It would seem that Kenny and Sumika have what it takes to overcome their problems and create a long-term, successful marriage. When they perceived they needed help, they actively sought out a supportive church community who could help them over the rough spots. They also began seeing a competent professional and Christian family counselor who is helping them understand their problems and resolve them with Christian love and forgiveness.

The birth of their second son, Lui, this past Valentine's Day has helped to bond them together even more closely. Several people in the church community stepped in to be neighborly during this stressful time—baby-sitting or doing various chores to help them get accustomed to the new baby.

So through prayer and the support of the church Sumika and Kenny have learned to trust God to help them with their marriage.

Kenny was the first person to suggest I write this book. It is my hope that by sharing these stories, many will be brought to new insights into their marriages—which in turn will serve as guideposts as they work at forging a happy, meaningful marriage in the years to come.

4

An American Mixed Marriage

Although Ken is a Caucasian with brown hair and Alice is a Japanese with black hair, they both grew up in America and therefore are both thoroughly "American".

When asked where they became acquainted, Ken answers, "We met in a bowling league we both belonged to. After knowing each other for about a year we began to think about marriage. Our marriage has lasted 32 years, but it was planned in the shortest time of any marriage I know of.

"One day we were out driving around and I said, 'Why

don't we drive over to Las Vegas and get married right away?' Alice didn't say anything. Then I said, 'I want you to say yes or no within the next two blocks.' She still didn't say anything, so I kept right on driving to Las Vegas and we got married. I suppose you could say our marriage was planned in less than five minutes. We got married on November 18, 1961."

"Our marriage had a rocky start," added Alice, "because my parents were unhappy about it. My sister had married a Caucasian and that marriage was not going too well, so they were wary about another interracial relationship. After a year we were reconciled with my parents—who invited us to have Thanksgiving dinner with them. Ever since then we have been on good terms with them."

"Yes," added Ken. "When Alice's father had a stroke we added a room on his house to make life easier for him—doing the work ourselves and providing all the materials."

"They appreciate the fact that our marriage has lasted over 30 years," said Alice, "especially since my sister's marriage didn't last half that long."

"That is not to say we haven't had our difficulties in our marriage—but it had nothing to do with our parents or with race," added Ken. "What really hurt us was my heavy drinking—which made life hard for both of us. I not only left Alice alone at home while I was hanging out in bars drinking, it finally almost killed me.

"One day I was trying to drive home but became so confused while driving my car that I didn't know where I was or where I was going. I finally stopped the car and got out to try to clear my head and find out where I was. All of a sudden I broke out in a cold sweat because I realized that if I had driven on for another 150 feet I would have driven off a cliff. That scared me. I made up my mind to stop drinking—and I have not had a drink in over five years."

"If he had not stopped I don't know if our marriage could have lasted this long," added Alice. "Many times I really got discouraged. But our love was strong enough to get us through until Ken finally quit drinking."

"What are some of the positive experiences you have shared that have kept you together?" I asked.

"Our son has turned out to be a real blessing for us," replied Ken. "He is a handsome young man of 29 now, but I must admit that when I first saw him I thought he was the ugliest baby I had ever seen. Fortunately he quickly grew out of that stage, and I'm anxiously waiting for him to hurry up and give us a grandchild—ugly or not!"

Alice said, "One good result of the marriage for me was that Ken led me to become a Christian. Before we got married I was not active in any religion, even though my parents were Buddhists. Now we enjoy our church life together—and have made some wonderful new friends here at our church."

"I don't know how much my Christian faith has helped to develop my value system," said Ken. "Maybe knowing God's love for me has helped me to love other people a little better. I certainly have more compassion and understanding toward others than I used to have.

"I am an expert pool player and many years ago I took advantage of my skill at pool to win a lot of money from my opponents. Finally I decided, 'Taking money from them may be taking food out of the mouths of their children.' After that I stopped ripping off amateurs. Alice and I both like golf, and we play quite often."

"Yes," said Alice. "I do like golf. And although we sometimes play together, I am glad that Ken doesn't complain when I spend a lot of time with my women golfing friends with whom I prefer to play. I think one thing that has helped our marriage succeed is that we do try to give each other some freedom to 'do our own thing'."

"I'm glad Alice has stuck by me, not only when I was drinking heavily but also now as my congestive heart problem grows worse." said Ken. "I have to take 527 pills a month just to keep going. And Alice knows I need all the help she can give me."

"If you had to give one main reason why your interracial marriage has succeeded, what would it be?" I asked.

Ken tapped his chest and said, "It is because of what we feel for one another inside here. How much of that comes from our Christian faith and how much of it may come from something else, I'm not sure. But we do care about each other and that has kept us together—in spite of some very rough times in our marriage."

Alice added, "We do love each other enough to try to adjust to one another's desires and needs. For example, it was Ken's love for me that led me to join in his church activities and Christian faith. Now he shows his love for me by coming with me to attend a Japanese-American church, although he is not Japanese."

Ken and Alice's marriage demonstrates their deep, abiding love for one another. This self-giving love and forgiving spirit they admit they have learned from Jesus Christ.

But there are also other factors which have made their interracial marriage easier. They do not have the problem of having to learn another language or adjust to a foreign culture. Since they both were born and grew up in America, they share a common history and heritage—albeit it with traditional variations.

Although the disapproval which came from Alice's parent's derived from their racial differences, their real difficulties came from Ken's drinking-related troubles. Learning to let each other "do their own thing" and adjusting to each other's needs were certainly boons to this marriage.

Alice must be commended for her steadfast dedication to the marriage which helped preserve it in spite of Ken's serious problems. Also by being willing to convert to Ken's Christian faith, she proved her love for Ken and for God.

Ken also worked to make their interracial marriage a success. He did not let the disapproval of Alice's parents embitter him against them, or towards Alice. He also recognized his shortcomings and exercised the tremendous discipline required to overcome his addictions. Although he says, "I did it for myself," still his love for Alice helped motivate him to do so.

Ken and Alice are not only a good example of how to make a mixed marriage succeed, but also an example of how to make any marriage succeed.

As Ken said, "Many people may view us as being different in race, but as for me there has never been any difference whatsoever. We have been raised in the same country with a common language and we are both equal to each other. Our simple humanity wipes away most of our differences and leaves us at the same starting point in terms of equality.

"No marriage could last," Ken continued, "if racial differences are continually emphasized. It is my faith in God which keeps me going in spite of serious health problems. And it is also faith in God that keeps our marriage going well."

5

The Foolish Rush

After having been a missionary in Japan for some 20 years, I was assigned to pastor a church near a co-ed English-speaking college. One day a Japanese student dashed into my church office and started pouring out his troubles to me in Japanese. He said, "I am in love with a Caucasian girl at the college. But her parents won't let us get married. They are prejudiced against me because I am Japanese."

Without waiting for me to respond he excitedly rushed on, "We must get married. I think about her morning, noon and night. I am making poor grades because I can't think of anything but this girl, Jane."

"Do your parents agree to the marriage?" I asked in Japanese.

"No, they don't want me to get married. But it is not because they are prejudiced. They just want me to forget about her and keep my mind on my studies. But I can never rest until I marry this girl!"

"You will have a lot of problems in the marriage if you

don't get both your parents to agree to it," I said. "Why don't you be patient. Perhaps they will agree when they see you love this girl enough to wait for her. Why not delay your marriage and keep trying to get both sets of parents to agree to it?" I suggested.

"But they are too prejudiced ever to agree," complained Kenji. Why can't they be like us Japanese? We aren't prejudiced toward anybody."

Seeing how despondent he was, I didn't tell him about the discrimination against Koreans and *Burakumin* (ghetto people) I had observed in Japan. Besides Kenji had only one thing on his mind and other people's problems would have to wait. This turned out to be the first of many counselling sessions that I had with both Kenji and Jane.

Since I taught part-time at the college, I asked their teachers about their school work. Jane's grades were poor and Kenji was failing most of his courses. He was a physical education major, but he didn't know English well enough to keep up with the other students. Beyond this, his emotional problems contributed to his failing grades. It seemed he was so infatuated with Jane he could concentrate on nothing else.

After many talks together, Kenji and Jane came into my office one day and said, "We now have the approval of our parents and want to get married right away. We think if we get married we can settle down and make better grades."

"Well," I replied, "if you now have approval from both your parents, and really think the marriage will help you to establish yourselves, I will ask the elders of our church about it. Since you are attending church regularly now they may agree to go ahead with it. You are both baptized Christians aren't you?"

"I am," answered Kenji. "I was baptized during a recent Baptist revival. It was a very emotional experience."

"If you are a Baptist why did you start coming to our Presbyterian church?" I asked. "Why not go to the Baptist minister and have him conduct your wedding?"

"He lives too far away," replied Kenji. "Besides, I don't like him any more. He gets me too upset."

"What about you, Jane?" I asked.

"Well," replied Jane, "I am attending your church because you are helping us. But neither I nor my folks have ever been church-going people. If you will marry us, I may become a Christian after that."

Although we all had some reservations about it, the elders and I finally agreed to have the wedding in our church. It was disappointing when none of the parents, and only a few of their college friends showed up for the wedding. Later we discovered that, in their eagerness to marry, they had deceived us. Their parents had not agreed to the marriage.

Their deception became clear when they never once returned to the church after the wedding. When I visited their rented apartment off campus they said, "We are married now. We no longer need you or the church. Don't visit us anymore. We don't want to be bothered."

Being barred from visiting them, I asked a retired missionary to Japan to try to help them in any way she could. This lady missionary was a member of our church and had met them several times. Later, this missionary helper came to me and said, "I have discovered some shocking things. Kenji and Jane admit that they deceived both us and their parents. They never got approval from their parents. Now their family relationships are deteriorating."

She continued with her report, "Jane's mother has said to her 'Don't you know that with Kenji's dark-brown skin you may have a "nigger" baby? We want you to leave him and come home at once. We will never allow that "Jap" into our home—even for a visit.' Naturally, both Kenji and Jane are very unhappy and upset. Although adults, they are acting like immature, spoiled children. I am really worried about them."

Some months later, my missionary friend reported, "Kenji and Jane now have a baby, but neither one wants to take care of it. The baby is being neglected. Also, they are deeply in debt. Kenji's folks still send money, and seem unaware that anything is wrong. Jane's folks have cut off her college expense money and refuse to help them in any way. Kenji had to take a job in a restaurant as a cook. To get there, he bought a car from another Japanese student but has never paid anything on it. I am afraid their life together is disintegrating and that unless a miracle happens their marriage is doomed."

Finally the dreaded report came, "Kenji has left Jane and transferred to another school. His parents still don't know anything about his failed marriage or his flunking out of this college—which is the real reason he had to transfer. Jane has gone back to her family with the baby, but none of them want it. They may give it to an adoption agency."

Surely their interracial differences contributed to the failure of this marriage, for it was their racism which prejudiced Jane's family against Kenji. The inability of this young couple to get their parents' approval did make the marriage more difficult. But, in the final analysis, it would seem fairer to blame the wrecked marriage on their character weaknesses. They had managed, in their young love, to overcome the problems of language and culture, but they stumbled over their own immaturity.

Basically it not that they were too dissimilar, but that Kenji and Jane were too much alike in their behavior patterns. Both were ruled by emotion more than by reason. Both were willing to deceive relatives and friends to get what they wanted. Both were so self-centered they could not make the sacrifices necessary to make the marriage succeed. Neither proved willing to care for a baby—or work out the other problems that plagued their marriage. Although adults, they were too immature to pay their debts or assume the responsibility for their decisions—let alone the consequences of their own actions.

The failure of this cross-cultural marriage thus can be laid at the feet of their infatuation with one another—and with their unwillingness to take advice. Without any true, lasting love for one another and with their emotional and intellectual immaturity, they found themselves in an isolated world of their own creation, bereft of any support group to help them over the rough spots. They jettisoned their religious commitment when it had served their purposes and also seemed to have abandoned any dependable value system.

This failed marriage also made me evaluate my part in this sad affair. With 20/20 hindsight, I realize I was too naïve and gullible. I let Kenji and Jane deceive me when they said their parents had agreed to the marriage. I was also mistaken in my belief that they were committed to the Christian vows they made at their wedding and failed to see they lacked a value system strong enough to make their marriage succeed. Together with the church elders, I had a false expectation that this young couple would continue coming to worship services where we could have been a support community to help them work out their problems.

Having suffered through this experience, I have been grateful for subsequent opportunities to be part of a support system that has helped other interracial marriages that did succeed. Also it is gratifying to discover, at least in my experience, that the successful ones far outnumbered the unsuccessful ones.

6

A Chinese-Japanese Love Story

Sam and Virginia Gin are an attractive young couple who a few years ago began attending the Japanese-American church where I serve part-time even though Sam is from a Chinese family background whereas Virginia is of Japanese descent.

When asked how they first met, Sam explained, "I was a supervisor for the Blue Cross Health Insurance System where I had a Chinese girl working for me by the name of Faith. Knowing I was approaching 30 and was still unmarried, Faith decided to make a helpful suggestion. 'I have a lovely Japanese friend named Virginia.' she said. 'Would you like to take her out to dinner and a movie?' Faith was a good friend and I knew she wouldn't recommend Virginia unless she was a likely prospect for a future bride. Therefore, I took her recommendation seriously. After I agreed, Faith set up a blind date for us. The rest is history.

"I liked her right off. Virginia was pretty and had a cheerful, outgoing personality. Since she was a school teacher, I knew she must be intelligent. And when she showed that she liked me, that proved she was very intelligent," said Sam, laughing.

When asked her first impression of Sam, Virginia replied, "I thought he was handsome, and, as he said about me, he had to be intelligent (because he liked me). Besides he had a good sense of humor, which I thought was important. In the many dates that followed, I found him to be kind hearted—and it was fun to do things together."

They dated for about a year before getting engaged and some six months later got married. When asked whether their respective Chinese and Japanese parents agreed to the marriage, Sam answered, "They not only agreed, but they urged us to do it sooner than we had planned. I guess they were worried because I was 31 by the time we married and Virginia was 27. Most of our relatives think people should marry at a younger age. But we both wanted to wait until the right person came along—and I'm glad we did. By that time we were mature enough to know what we wanted in a marriage partner. I think that is one reason why our marriage has been a good one."

"Were you both active Christians when you married?" I asked.

"No," replied Virginia, "Sam had been quite active in a church as a young boy, but I had never attended a church regularly until after we married. But we were married in a Christian church."

"How do you feel your Christian beliefs have helped your marriage?" I inquired.

Virginia replied, "Our relationship to Christ and his church has helped our marriage in several ways. It has given us a deeper understanding of what love and forgiveness is all about. And most marriages need a lot of both of those to succeed. If our love didn't include forgiveness we could never get along as well as we do. And sharing in the fellowship and support we find at church also helps us as a family."

"I'll never forget some of the happy times we have had in church together," said Sam. "We were married in the Oneonta Congregational Church in South Pasadena, California. I remember the wonderful feeling that came over me when Reverend Mr. Roberts said, 'You are now husband and wife. You may kiss the bride.'

"Of course I had enjoyed a few kisses before that, but this one was special. It meant we were promising to love and support each other as long as we lived. Our life together since that day has been blessed. Just four months after the wedding, we were able to buy our first home—in Glendale. After Samantha was added to our family, we were able to buy an even larger home in San Marino where we now live."

Virginia added, "And of course we can't forget the happy additions we've had. I'll never forget that wonderful event—the birth of our first child, Amy. This was repeated three years later when Samantha was born, and then again two years later with the birth of our son, Gregory."

"Do your children think of themselves as Chinese, Japanese or just plain American?" I asked.

"I would say, just plain American," replied Sam. "Like us, they are proud of both their Chinese and Japanese connections, but they don't try to emphasize either of them. Since they were born and raised in America, speak English and follow American customs, they don't think our interracial marriage is such a big deal."

"Do they speak any Chinese or Japanese?" I inquired.

"Yes," replied Sam. "They speak a little Japanese and Chinese sometimes—when they are with their grandparents. But English is definitely their main language."

"Have they ever had to face any prejudice because of being Oriental?" I asked.

"No, I don't think so," replied Sam. "But they may have faced some subtle types of prejudice that I am not aware of."

"Then, you don't feel that there are any disadvantages in being a cross-cultural couple?" I asked.

"On the contrary," replied Sam. "We see our interracial marriage as having many advantages. We get to know something about both Japanese and Chinese culture. Our horizons are broadened by contact with these two Oriental cultures. Someday, we would like to visit both Japan and China—if we can ever afford the time and money required to do that."

"Have you had any unhappy times in your life together?" I asked.

"Not really," replied Virginia, "except that Sam has had some trouble with high blood pressure for the past few years. I worry about that, and especially the bad side effects his medication can have. We just hope and pray that he will continue to be healthy. Since Sam owns and operates his own business now, he has to deal with a lot of responsibility and daily pressure. That's why I can't help but worry about his health."

"What is his business?" I asked.

"It is called ENL Business Consultants," replied Virginia. "He advises business people—trying to help make his clients' businesses more successful."

"Do you also work outside the home?" I asked Virginia.

"Yes," replied Virginia. "I have a part-time job in our local school system. I also do a lot of volunteer work in the PTA programs at our children's schools. It keeps me hopping—especially since I have to keep up a home for our family of five at the same time. Thankfully, Sam and the children do give me some help."

"What do you two see as the essence of a good marriage?" I asked.

Sam replied, "When we marry we have to learn to transform our individual goals into partnership or family goals. If personal goals aren't compatible with your partner's goals you have to be willing to reconsider them. You need to determine what is best for the family—now and in the future. Each partner needs to be patient and understanding about the other partner's desires and needs. No marriage is an automatic success. Both partners must be loving and flexible as they work out what is best for their marriage and family."

How can we evaluate the cross-cultural aspect of Sam and Virginia's marriage? They certainly have some admirable insights into marriage and each other—which they learned from their respective cultures. It would appear that they have gleaned important lessons from their cultures and built a strong relationship based on mutual love and respect. Besides they obviously enjoy each other and their life together.

Their children also reflect their family-centered value system.

They are bright and pleasant additions to the Sunday school program. In all aspects, this cross-cultural family seems to me to be an example of what a Christian family should be.

7

A Thai-Filipino Shared Ministry

Joe and Gloria's interracial marriage set a speed record hard to beat. Three weeks after their first date they were engaged. Two months later they got married—in Claremont, California at the church where they first met. Although there were a few rough spots at the beginning, they have now been successfully married for 22 years and have two smart, good-looking children.

When I first asked them how they had met, Joe, being a Christian gentleman and pastor, let Gloria have the first word.

She explained, "I first saw Joe when I went to my sister's church and saw this handsome man sitting in the choir. I said to her, 'I hope he is a Filipino. Who knows, maybe he is the guy the Lord wants me to marry.' As he went by our pew during the choir's recessional my sister's daughter said, 'He's good looking.' As a well-trained Asian girl I restrained my enthusiasm and answered, 'Not bad.' I saw Joe briefly then, but I had to keep a tight lid on my feelings for two more months before I finally got to talk to him."

Joe added, "I was also attracted to Gloria from the first time I saw her but I finally got a chance to talk to her—because I needed to ask a favor of her younger sister. My Thai niece wanted to come to study in the U.S. and I heard that Gloria's younger sister was secretary to the head of the international students program at Chapman College in Orange, California. Our first date was when Gloria drove me to Chapman College in her 1968 Mustang. Sparks began to fly between us from that first encounter."

"Yes," added Gloria. "We took my sister to lunch that day because it was her birthday. At lunch my fortune cookie said, 'A good chance to go abroad with a future life partner.' I blushed (if ever you could see through my dark brown skin) from head to toe. I was embarrassed, yet feeling more secure that maybe this is indeed the man God has been reserving for me. Hearing my fortune cookie prediction, Joe also seemed shook up. Anyway, the romance started that day—and in three weeks we bought an engagement ring."

"How did your parents, and other family members, feel about the marriage?" I asked.

"Well," said Joe. "My father was no longer living, but I was a little worried about whether my mother would agree. I wrote her, saying that I planned to marry a girl who is not a Thai, but who has the same dark brown skin that I have. Her answer didn't come for over two months, and by that time we were already married. I was greatly relieved when she wrote, 'I am happy the girl you are marrying is a Christian. And I have always wanted you to marry a nurse like Gloria, because you were often sick when you were a little boy. I pray that God will bless your marriage.' My youngest sister objected, because some of her Thai friends wanted to marry me. Later she wrote Gloria a beautiful letter saying, 'I have learned to not only like you but love you'."

"There was no problem with my family," said Gloria. "My parents were in Chicago on their way to visit my four brothers and two sisters who live in America, and they joyfully came to the wedding. They were greatly relieved that their 31-year-old daughter was finally getting married. For the wedding my family all pitched in to help prepare the traditional egg rolls and noodles (pansit) for the reception, and my younger sister was the Maid of Honor."

When asked about his upbringing in Thailand, Joe explained, "My Thai father was a Buddhist monk, converted to Christianity by my Christian mother. Eventually, my father became a Christian minister but died suddenly, a few months after beginning his ministry. Wanting to fulfill his unfinished ministry was an important factor which led me finally to become a Christian minister myself after having spent several years as a Christian teacher in schools in Thailand. It was when I came to study at the Claremont School of Theology that I met Gloria."

Gloria pointed out the similarities with her life in the

Philippines. "My father was also a Christian minister in the Philippines, and my mother had to work hard to help support our large family of twelve children—of which I was number eleven. Somehow they managed to send all of their children to Silliman University (a Christian university in the Philippines) and on to other universities in the Philippines and in the U.S. Out of the twelve, they have produced two medical doctors, two nurses, one minister, two teachers, one lawyer, one engineer and one agriculturist.

"I came to America on a visit, but stayed on here when my sister persuaded me to take a nursing job at the famous City of Hope Hospital in Duarte, California. My father is proud that his son-in-law, Joe, joined him in the Christian ministry."

"What are some of the problems you have faced in your interracial marriage?" I asked.

"One problem," said Joe, "was that when we first got married neither of us knew the other's first language or native customs. Not knowing each other's culture made us see things from a different point of view—resulting in one big disagreement just a week before our marriage. It was so serious we considered calling off the wedding, but we decided we were meant for each other.

"For us we have found that the misunderstandings due to differences in culture and in the way we differ in our thinking can be resolved by taking on a third way. For both of us, having lived in America for several years was a real blessing. We found we could communicate well in English and live harmoniously by following American customs. We were even able to overcome a 'fight' we had on our honeymoon."

"One big problem for me," said Gloria, "was that our ministry had to be carried on in the Thai language. I tried to learn it but I couldn't hear the five tones that the Thai language has. My Philippine Cebuano language isn't a tonal system. Sitting in groups where everyone was speaking the Thai language that I couldn't understand, made me feel very isolated and lonely.

"Before we married I told Joe I would go with him to Thailand, but I'm glad we stayed here. However, I was willing to have our two children learn Thai instead of my Filipino language, because we need Thai in our church work. I felt it was right for me to give up my Filipino language and culture to help our ministry with Thai people to succeed. I even learned to like the spicy, hot Thai food. Filipino food seems bland now."

"Another problem," said Joe, "was that we had our parents living with us for several years. Gloria's mother and father lived here in their eighties and nineties and my mother lived with us at the same time, for three years. She was in her seventies. Neither could understand the other's language, so most of their communication was carried on with smiles and sign language. One good benefit of that was that our children learned Thai from their grandmother, who could speak neither English nor Filipino. Children can learn a language much faster than an adult."

"One of the things I really like about Joe," said Gloria, "is that, unlike most Asian men, he helps a lot with the housework. He does more cooking than I do. As a minister, he can arrange most of his own schedule and he usually has our dinner ready by the time I get home from my hospital nursing job. Since he helps with the work, I don't mind when he has Thai visitors, or other friends, in our home. He also handles our finances."

"What was the most unhappy time in your marriage?" I asked.

"For me," answered Gloria. "It was the time Joe was operating a Thai restaurant to help supplement our income. At that time the Thai church was too small to pay Joe a good salary. Joe was working too hard and I had to help with the restaurant at night, after a full day's work at the hospital. We were both so tired we didn't even have the energy to carry on our usual disagreements and 'fights'. I was grateful when the church became self-supporting and able to pay Joe a good salary."

"How did the Thai church first get started?" I asked.

"In 1973 with the help of a Korean missionary couple who had served in Thailand, I and another friend started the Thai Church in Hollywood," said Joe. "In 1981 we decided to affiliate with the Presbyterian Church (USA) because most of our members were from that background in Thailand. In 1989 our Thai Community Church moved to El Monte and it is now known as the First Thai Presbyterian Church in the U.S.A. Soon we will celebrate our twenty-first anniversary."

"I'm sure you are both happy about the success of your shared ministry with Thai people in the U.S. What other highlights do you identify as having been a product of your interracial marriage?" I asked.

"Of course, one of the happiest," said Joe, "was the birth of our daughter. Baby Joy became a real 'joy' in my life and I loved taking care of her. Since my Thai mother lived with us for three years, Joy learned both English and Thai languages. Then four years later the birth of our son, David, was an added blessing. And I am happy Gloria and I have had 22 good years together, in spite of my hot temper, and we are growing closer every year. God has really blessed our marriage and our shared ministry."

"What are the basic ingredients for a successful marriage?" I asked.

"In my opinion," answered Gloria, "there are at least four basic elements. There has to be a give and take from both sides. Of course, love is the greatest ingredient, and it is to our love that I attribute the solidarity of our marriage. Paul advised husbands to love their wives as much as Jesus loved the church. I think my husband has lived up to this ideal 100%, because he has always made me feel loved by him. He is also a good provider. As a wife, I am to honor my husband which I have tried hard to do. But when I have failed he forgave me. And I, too, have learned to forgive. You will notice these ingredients apply not only to interracial marriages but to all marriages. If these ingredients are there, I don't think differences in race or culture really matter. They can be overcome."

"What do you see as the major advantage of an interracial marriage?" I asked.

Gloria responded, "The major advantage of an interracial marriage is getting to know another culture. That is not only interesting, it broadens one's horizons. Some of my happiest moments in life have been being with friends and loved ones in Thailand while on vacation there. We seem always to want to go there for vacation, because we see our family—and besides, it is less expensive with the good dollar exchange rate there so our vacation dollar goes farther. Moreover, it is a beautiful country with nice people. I consider it to be a blessing in my life to be married to someone from Thailand."

How can we evaluate the interracial marriage of Gloria and Joe? I think they have summarized it well with their marriage views and loving relationship. The basic reason for their successful marriage is contained in a letter, signed by both of them. They wrote: "We believe that marriage has to be grounded on Jesus Christ who is the source of love that binds us all together. He is also our source of strength in times of weakness, and source of power in times of temptation. Like Joshua, our home motto is, 'But as for me and my household, we will serve the Lord' (Josh 13:15). We are committed to serve the Lord and to stay married. Thanks be to God through our Lord Jesus Christ that he is alive in the person of the Holy Spirit—who can change us to be better persons if we only ask of him through prayer. Nothing is impossible with God."

Joe and Gloria provide a wonderful role model for the church to use—in our efforts to help other interracial couples live Christ-centered, happy lives.

8

Irreconcilable Differences

Ben and Debbie started coming to a church I served in Tennessee. He was a red-headed Caucasian, she a small, dark Filipino. On the surface their interracial marriage seemed to be going reasonably well. There were a few hints of trouble—signs we should have been able to recognize earlier.

Ben was very protective toward Debbie—and a little domineering. He seemed to disapprove of her every now and then—as if she was not meeting his ideal of what a wife should be. And he seemed to treat her more like a "daughter" than a wife.

Nevertheless, it was a complete surprise to me when he came into my office one day and announced, "I have decided to divorce my wife. And I want you to agree to it." He gave no reasons for his decision. Later I learned that one reason he had left his family's Baptist church to come to our Presbyterian one was that he knew his Baptist pastor was always against any divorce. Ben was hoping our Presbyterian community would be more lenient.

My immediate question was, "Are you sure you are doing

what is best for both of you? Have you discussed your problems or tried to resolve them with the help of any marriage counseling program?"

I was surprised when Ben explained that though he had thought about divorce for a long time, he had never discussed it with Debbie or with anyone else. I thought this less than fair and suggested that his first step should be to talk to Debbie openly about his feelings and then seek out some counseling to see if they could resolve their problems in a way that would save their marriage.

Reluctantly, as if he resented the delay, Ben finally agreed to come with Debbie to at least talk with me for a few counseling sessions—even though I considered myself hardly well enough trained to do an adequate job as a marriage counselor. In seminary we were given one course in pastoral counseling—which coupled together with reading some books on counseling hardly prepared me to help people, including interracial couples, get over the rocky spots in their paths. But Ben refused to go elsewhere, so I tried at least to listen to their woes.

During those sessions they explained their history. While serving with the military in the Philippines Ben met Debbie and felt attracted to her. At the time she was in poor health and he felt he could help her and protect her. Because of her weak heart, her family treated her specially, never requiring her to do the housework and other duties her sisters did. Being able to rescue this helpless girl seemed to be Ben's main motive for wanting to marry Debbie. At first her family objected, citing her poor health, but they were finally convinced and gave their blessing.

When Ben was released from the military, he brought

Irreconcilable Differences

Debbie to his hometown in Tennessee where he got a good job with the TVA. Although her health greatly improved in America, Debbie never seemed able to break the pattern of acting helpless and letting Ben function as her "protector".

But this role became tiresome and one of Ben's chief complaints was that, following Filipino customs, Debbie spent much of their sizable income entertaining Filipino friends who lived in the area. Ben recognized her actions as following Filipino customs but he still resented it—especially as Debbie used her "poor health" as an excuse not to entertain guests at home, so they spent lavish amounts entertaining her Filipino guests in restaurants or providing "take out" food for meetings in their home.

Ben felt that since Debbie's health was now so improved—she felt good enough to complete a course of training as a beautician—she could do more cooking and housecleaning. But even when they had no guests they ate most of their meals out and she hired someone to do her housework. He complained, "I want to save and invest our money and Debbie wants to spend all of it. Her ideas and mine are poles apart." The old "protector and protected" pattern was growing thin. Debbie still liked being coddled, but Ben was tired of spending all his money indulging her.

Worst of all, neither would openly discuss their feelings and problems with the other. Although the Filipino Tagalog language was her native tongue, like most Filipinos, Debbie was trained in English and had no problem in that language, so this was not the real barrier. The barrier that made their communicate difficult was psychological. They really had never gotten to the core of their differences about children.

Ben wanted a family, but Debbie wasn't so sure. Although

most Filipinos have large families, Debbie seemed hesitant about having children. Her earlier ill health certainly was a factor, but it also seemed she was reluctant to give up her comfortable life-style to be saddled with the care of a baby. Her misgivings seemed to be a component in their not having a good physical relationship, yet she seemed to feel guilty she couldn't overcome this negative attitude. It was an unhappy situation for both of them.

One day Debbie came to me and said, with forced gaiety I thought, "I'm pregnant! Isn't that great!" I agreed with her even though her attitude made me uncomfortable. When she had a miscarriage a few weeks later, she seemed greatly relieved. In contrast Ben was crushed by the tragedy. Because of her Roman Catholic background Debbie was indignant when someone suggested she had "aborted" the baby. "It was not an abortion," said Debbie angrily. "It was only a miscarriage!"

This loss of the baby seemed to be the last straw for Ben who seemed to give up any hope of saving their marriage. One of our elders in the church was a lawyer who handled many divorce cases. In discussing this with him, he said, "I agree that divorce is never a good thing but, in many cases, it is better than keeping two miserable people in a marriage that has failed. Sometimes two people are just not compatible enough to have a successful marriage—and when that happens it seems better to be supportive of the divorce. That way you can continue to counsel with them after the divorce to help them make the adjustment."

Ben tried to be "fair" in the divorce, but I noticed he insisted that he keep the home. He gave Debbie one of the family cars and a reasonable financial settlement.

Irreconcilable Differences

Using her beautician's training, Debbie took a job in a nearby beauty parlor, proving she could be independent—when forced to do so. She stopped coming to church, so I stopped by for a haircut to see her. She acted rather nervous and my presence seemed to trigger so many negative feelings I wondered whether I should have stayed away. Finally she said, while cutting my hair, "You know, I didn't want the divorce, but I guess my not being a very good wife and housekeeper may have helped to cause it. Maybe I am at least partly to blame for the divorce. I should have done more for Ben."

Even though the divorce was tragic, I was encouraged to see Debbie's newfound independence and improved ability to evaluate herself realistically. It appears being forced to take care of her own affairs has helped improve her self-image.

What can we learn from the failure of this cross-cultural marriage? Certainly part of their problems was due to racial and cultural differences. Debbie's Filipino custom of spending her husband's money lavishly entertaining Filipino friends contributed tensions to the relationship, but it would seem their real affliction centered more on their differences in personality and values. He was a saver and investor, she was a spender. Unlike most Filipino wives who are good cooks, housekeepers and sexual partners, Debbie allowed her earlier illness to excuse her personal dislike of housework and other familial responsibilities. Then, Ben rejected her like a "house pet" he had wearied of. And neither seemed to be willing to change or adjust to new roles that would have saved their marriage.

Regrettably, neither seemed to have the self-giving love and forgiving spirit we all need to make a marriage successful. Although nominal Christians, neither Ben nor Debbie were willing to fling themselves on Christ's mercy to allow Jesus to help them save their marriage.

An interesting sequel to this saga was a letter I received from Ben some two years after the divorce. He reported he was trying out his third denomination and was now planning a second interracial marriage. He wrote, "I have found a wonderful new prospective bride in Honduras. She is from a poor family, but she is young, healthy and a good housekeeper. She is eager to marry me and come to the U.S.A. We are planning to marry as soon as I can work out her immigration papers."

Ben gave her age as 18, compared to his 40—young enough to be his daughter. This was the last I heard from Ben. But I still wonder about his new marriage and why he had to go to Honduras to find a new wife. Is he reviving his old "protector and protected" roles? All we can do is pray that God will help this new marriage to succeed.

As for Debbie, when last seen, she was working successfully as a beautician, enjoying her new sense of independence and has a much better understanding of her own self-worth. She seems to have no plans to return to the Philippines, or even to marry again. They both remain in my prayers.

9

Witnessing Together in Korea

Art Kinsler was born in Korea to missionary parents. After college and seminary training in America, Art returned to Korea as a missionary. Having lived in Korea for many years, Art felt at home there. But it was not until he was 30 that he met an attractive Korean woman who became his wife. The first time they met, Art was impressed by Sue's long black hair and dark eyes, but he was even more struck by her bright smile and gentle ways.

They met in a church where Art was working and Sue was

visiting her friend, the organist there. At first there was only a small spark of romance between them, but over the next three years of meeting and dating, they fell in love and finally decided to marry in the Chapel of the Tai Hwa Methodist Social Center in Seoul, Korea—which was crowded with relatives and friends from Korea and America.

From the beginning Art's parents approved of the marriage although, at first, Sue's parents had misgivings. Her father was won over after he had a long talk with Art and his father before the wedding, but her mother was worried because her 22-year-old daughter was marrying a man twelve years her senior. Sue's mother was gratified when she saw how well the marriage was going, and was fully won over when Sue and Art produced a fine grandson for her.

Art and Sue came from disparate backgrounds and have weathered some difficult storms but they have what can be considered a successful interracial marriage.

When asked about her family, Sue answered, "My father was a successful businessman in Korea and I grew up in a prosperous home with one sister and four brothers. At age 15, I was the first in my family to become a Christian. Later my younger sister became a Christian and married the son of a Korean minister. My younger brother is active in the church. Two other brothers attended for a while but don't go to church now. My father became a Christian just before his death, but my mother still hasn't been able to make that decision. I am still praying for her."

When asked whether being married to a Korean helps make his ministry in Korea more effective, Art replied, "Definitely. Simply because since Sue is Korean, she can explain Korean customs to me that I can't perceive and she helps me with language problems. She is a wonderful pastor's wife and a real boon as a co-worker in our mission work."

"What other advantages come your way from your interracial marriage?" I asked.

Art said, "Being an interracial couple, we meet many interesting people and have a wider range of experiences because we have contacts with two cultures. We also have a richer ministry together than we could have working separately."

Sue added, "At first our interracial marriage seemed to be a disadvantage to me. I didn't know the English language very well and I didn't know American customs—or how to cook American foods. I never visited America until after our marriage. Now that I know more about American customs and can speak English, I see many advantages for me and our children. My life is richer, and our two boys, John and Ross, appreciate having the benefit of two languages and two cultures."

"Yes," added Art, "and now she is a good cook for both Korean and American food. But I must admit that when I'm in the U.S., I would rather eat an American breakfast."

"And I must confess," said Sue," that one of my most unhappy experiences in our early married life was due to Art's dislike of some Korean foods. One day I worked hard to make a special Korean dish and was totally crushed when instead of appreciating all my hard labor, he turned up his nose and said, 'What in the world is *that*?' I'm glad he now has learned to like many Korean dishes."

"What challenges have you faced in your marriage?" I asked.

"The most difficult thing in our life" answered Art, "was when, after having two fine healthy boys, our third child, Elaine, was born with physical and mental handicaps. Although

Elaine is now 16, mentally she is about age three. This situation has been hard for both of us."

"Yes," added Sue. "Taking care of Elaine at home for ten years kept me very busy. But, thankfully, through caring for her I was given a sympathy and concern for all handicapped people. Later I was able to develop a ministry to handicapped people in Korea—which is a great need because there is a temptation for some Koreans from a Buddhist background to neglect handicapped children thinking their problems are a result of 'karma', or a 'punishment' for having done something bad in a previous incarnation. Thankfully, as Christianity grows in Korea, this attitude of seeing handicapped children as a 'shameful burden' is changing and my ministry to the handicapped has been very rewarding."

Sue continued, "When Elaine was two, I began this ministry by helping with the handicapped young people who were enrolled at the Vocational Training School next door to us in Soonchon, Korea. Most of them had received rehabilitative surgery at the Presbyterian Hospital and were learning dressmaking. I assisted in preparing them for holding down a needed job. Later when we moved to Seoul, I worked with over a hundred vocational school graduates and this ministry developed into what we now call a 'Koinonia Sheltered Workshop' for handicapped people. We have 26 handicapped people working in the sewing factory there with 15 of them living in the related dormitory. Now, with Elaine living in a special group home and attending special education classes in Riverside, California, I have even more time to devote to this ministry."

"What are some of the rewarding experiences you have had in working with the handicapped?" I asked.

"One happy experience for both of us," Art replied, "was using our home in Korea for the wedding of two handicapped couples. For one wedding we expected some 30 people to come into our home, but ended up with over 120 crowded in."

"My happiest experience," said Sue, "was helping to heal and save a handicapped man. For twelve years he had been receiving the wrong treatment because everyone thought he had T.B. (tuberculosis). Thinking he was at death's door, he asked me to visit him. After helping Mr. Lee accept Jesus and praying for healing, his severe bleeding stopped for nine days. At this point I managed to get him admitted to a local Christian hospital where they found his real problem was a lung tumor. Twelve days after removing the tumor he was recovered. A week later he was back at work. It was like a miracle from God. Christ had brought him from 'darkness to light' (Jn 8:12) and he and his wife finally had the baby son they had longed for. Subsequently most of his relatives became Christians. In fact, to my joy, because of Mr. Lee many other handicapped people have become Christians through our ministry to them."

When asked about the highlights in his ministry, Art thought a minute and then said, "Our ministry has been very blessed. For example, through our church contacts we have been able to help many interracial couples solve some of their problems. In this, as in most of our church ministry, we find we are more effective because we represent two cultures. Also I appreciate how well we complement each other in our ministry—I being the 'analytical' one and Sue the 'feeling' one.

"I think one of my happiest experiences in the ministry was helping to develop a much-needed church for working people in an industrial area in Korea. That church has brought the light of Jesus Christ into the lives of people who desperately need it."

"Regarding cultural differences, have you had to work out any disagreement in your own marriage?" I asked.

"Oh yes," replied Art. "When our first baby was born Sue insisted on putting the baby to sleep on its back—a Korean custom. I wanted to put the baby to sleep on its stomach—an American custom. We also had different customs regarding the entertainment of guests. Sue's friends just dropped by anytime, without telling us ahead of time—a Korean custom. My friends and I usually set up visits at least a week in advance—an American custom. But, with Christian love and consideration on both sides we try to work out some mutually agreeable compromise regarding cultural differences. As I have said many times, interracial marriage is a 'high risk—high gain' experience for most couples."

"Which do you think is harder to overcome, cultural differences or personality differences?" I asked.

"Well," replied Art. "Sometimes, when we are having trouble understanding each other, we are not sure whether it is due to one or the other. Probably both contribute to our differences. The important thing is to pray together, as we often do in family devotions, and let God help us to work through our problems, no matter what caused them. Prayer, and God's help, have been the most important things in making our interracial marriage a success."

"Do your children feel more at home in Korea or in America?" I asked.

Art replied, "Our children pretty much identify with both cultures and languages, although English is dominant because they attended American schools. When small, their friends would ask about their parents and they would answer proudly, 'My father is American and my mother is Korean.' Also our family really feels at home in both Korea and America, or perhaps I should say 'half at home' in both countries. Because in both countries either Sue or I are 'native citizens', our children identify with either."

"Have you faced much prejudice in either Korea or America?" I asked.

Art answered, "Because I was a pastor and missionary, born of missionary parents in Korea, the usual Korean prejudice against interracial marriages was something we did not experience. Of course in both countries there would sometimes be comments or incidents that were less than happy, but these didn't bother us. In our interracial marriage counseling we often had to explain Korean prejudices to Americans and American prejudices to Koreans. Our children have experienced virtually no prejudice and enjoy friendships with many Asian students at their American university."

"What advice do you give to interracial couples you counsel?" I asked.

Art answered, "We tell them: 'Make sure you understand the importance and sanctity of marriage; then work together to meet the challenges of marriage; be flexible regarding adjustments that have to be made for jobs, relatives, and where you live; find supportive friends; and, above all, find the spiritual help from God that all of us need'."

Certainly Art and Sue's experience show what a boon it is for a foreign missionary to have a spouse who grew up in that country who understands the nuances of that culture and can be of exceptional service in forging a ministry that meets the real needs of their own people, rather than the foreigner's "perceived needs".

Their experience also shows that with God's help an interracial couple can turn a diversity like a handicapped child, into a new ministry that merges solutions that have come from both cultural experiences. Watching Art and Sue trying to teach handicapped Elaine to swim, I was deeply impressed by their patience and obvious love for her. They are good role models in whatever culture they find themselves.

As we parted, we prayed together and I thought, "That is the real key to the success of this interracial marriage—their dependence on the Holy Spirit to help them overcome every problem they face."

10

Happiness Is Where You Find It

Linda, a lovely, dark-haired woman from Indonesia married Richard, a tall, handsome French-Canadian ten years ago. They settled in California where they have since added two delightful children to their family. We met when they sought out our Japanese-American church for their church home even though they are outnumbered by Japanese-Americans about 100 to one.

When I asked them what they had in common Richard replied, "Many things. We are both Christians, we both like people, we are both well educated, we have a common interest in music and our ethical and moral values are similar. We both understand the responsibilities of a husband and wife to one another, and our common responsibility to our children."

Linda spoke up saying, "Although I am attending college to become a civil engineer, I can manage my schoolwork because I get a lot of help at home from Richard. He is self-employed, repairing and selling pianos and old cars, which means he can work out of our home and is often here to share in our child-care and housekeeping duties."

"What are some of the problems you have had to face as a mixed marriage family?" I asked.

"It was a little hard to communicate at first," admitted Richard, "because we grew up with different languages and cultures. Now we do pretty well, because we have shared the English language and American culture for ten years. Growing up in Montreal, Canada my first language was French. It was tough at first. I expected Linda to know how I felt about things as a Canadian-American and she expected me to understand her feelings as an Indonesian woman. There didn't seem to be words to explain to each other what we felt, because I didn't know Indonesian and she was just learning English.

"In fact we met when she was taking ESL (English as a second language) courses in Alhambra. I'm glad she knows English well now. It makes our life together much easier."

Linda added, "After all, if you know enough to say 'I love you' in each other's language the rest of the problems can be worked out." She laughed brightly, "It's hard to live so far away from my family. I had to force myself to stay in American for the birth of our children. It would have been comforting to go back to be with my mother for that, but we have our children now, and Richard's family has been kind to me."

"In your opinion, what is necessary to have a good interracial marriage?" I asked.

"Understanding each other's language and culture is essential," replied Richard. "But I also think having compatible personalities and similar values is more important than having the same race or language. After all, the divorce rate among people with the same language and culture is very high—when they don't have compatible personalities or values."

"Is marrying a person of another race an advantage or a disadvantage to marriage?" I asked.

Linda answered, "If you have a happy marriage, really love each other and can appreciate a foreign culture, the differences can actually be an advantage. Sharing life with a person from another race and culture can enrich the marriage—bringing new and interesting ideas and information into their life. At least that is true for me."

"I agree," added Richard. "Learning about Linda's Indonesian culture has certainly brought new ideas and values into my life. I have visited Indonesia with her three times since our marriage. My horizons are much wider than they were before we met. And being from another race, Linda has taught me to be more sensitive to and appreciative of all other races. I must admit, that Indonesian culture is difficult to understand, because it is such a mixture of Muslim, Christian and Hindu influences."

"Actually," said Linda, "we have more trouble working out our financial problems and finding time to spend together than any trouble that comes from being from different cultures." She added, "One thing I do like about the American culture is that husbands are more likely to help with the housework than in

Indonesia. Also American supermarkets and the prepared foods available everywhere make housekeeping easier here."

"What are some of the things that have helped to make your marriage a success?" I asked.

Richard replied, "We do work together to try to solve the problems that come up in our marriage. For example, I am very individualistic and Linda emphasizes family ties more than I do. But we have learned to compromise about such differences. We know we're not perfect, and since I'm not perfect, I can't expect Linda to be. Since we believe in Christian love and forgiveness, we can forgive mistakes and harsh words of criticism that may hurt us. We do try to avoid 'tender spots' when we discuss our problems. Sometimes we postpone discussion until we have time to cool off and see things more objectively."

"How have your values and religious ideas changed and developed since your marriage?" I inquired.

"Well," replied Richard. "Linda was a more dedicated Christian than I was when we first met. Many things, including the recession and our financial problems, have made me revise my religious views. I now know that materialism and humanism are not enough. We need God's guidance and help to work out our problems and needs. That's why I started going to church with Linda and our children."

Linda added, "As Christians, my parents were upset when we started living together in 1983. But after we got married two years later, our family relationships got much better. As I mentioned earlier, I'm grateful God gave me the strength to stay with Richard for the birth of our children and not give in to my desire to go back to Indonesia to be with my family for that important event. God can help us to stay together, and support each other, even when it is hard to do."

"How do you feel about the problems of marriage, and the problems of divorce?" I asked.

"Let's face it—marriage presents many problems," replied Richard, "but divorce may present even greater problems. For example, what to do about the children, the house, the jobs and income problems. It is easier to take care of household duties, and expenses, when two are there to help. Single parenthood is much tougher than most people think it is."

"Does that mean you are optimistic about the future of your interracial marriage?" I asked.

"Yes," replied Richard. "It is hard to raise two children, and we have financial problems. But I believe that, with God's help, our marriage will continue to be good—but we must both be willing to keep working out our problems together."

This seemed like wise counsel for all relationships. Certainly their Christian commitment plus their openness about their problems and their strengths bodes well for the future of this interracial marriage.

11

Bridging Traditional Animosities

Keith Takeshita was excited about his new job as an accountant at a company in his native Hawaii. What he didn't expect was to meet a lovely co-worker whom he couldn't get off his mind. From her pretty black hair, dark eyes and Oriental features he knew she must be either Japanese, Chinese or Korean, but he didn't know which.

He soon learned her name was Cindy, but he was reticent to ask her any personal questions. It was a long time before he felt they knew each other well enough for him to screw up his

Happiness Is Where You Find It

courage and inquire, "Where are you from, Cindy?"

"I was born and grew up in Korea," answered Cindy. "Recently our family moved here to Hawaii."

"Could I meet your family someday?" asked Keith. "I want them to like me. Since I am from a Japanese background, I know some Koreans don't like the Japanese—because of Japan's harsh rule over Korea in the past."

Cindy laughed and said, "I would be happy to introduce you to my family. You are a Japanese-American. My family certainly wouldn't dislike you. And I am sure that you know Korea and Japan are becoming more friendly now."

When Keith eventually got to meet Cindy's mom, he was pleased at the good rapport they seemed to establish from the beginning. Cindy's mom couldn't speak much English and he didn't know Korean, but they still found ways to communicate—without Cindy having to translate—with smiles, handshakes and sign language.

One night Keith and Cindy came home from a date. Worried that Keith had a long trip home over 30 miles of dark and dangerous roads, Cindy's mom asked her in Korean, "Do you think Keith might want to spend the night here? We could get out the extra mattress and have him sleep on the floor."

When this was translated for Keith, he couldn't believe how much Cindy's mom had come to like him and trust him for he knew she never extended such a privilege to any of Cindy's older sisters' Korean boyfriends. "Thank you!" said Keith enthusiastically. "That would be greatly appreciated."

Keith's gentle manner and handsome face had won the approval of both Cindy and her mom. After a long courtship Keith decided he did indeed love this attractive Korean girl and wanted to marry her. He picked what he hoped was the right moment and said, "I love you Cindy. Will you marry me?"

Cindy smiled her beautiful smile and said, "I do want to marry you, but give me a little more time to think it over and make sure my family agrees."

Cindy's family consented to the marriage, as did Keith's father, but Keith's mother was not pleased. "I want you to marry your own kind!" she said. "Why can't you find a nice Japanese girl to marry?"

Later, when she discovered Keith had kept secret the fact that Cindy was two years older than he, she really got upset. "Not only are you marrying a Korean girl, you are marrying an older woman! Don't you know the woman is supposed to be *younger* than the man? All three of your sisters know that. Why does my only son have to disappoint me like this?"

"I apologize for breaking a family tradition," responded Keith. "But race and a two-year age difference are not important to me. Please understand how I feel and agree to the marriage, Mom."

Keith was grateful when eventually she did come around—thanks to his father's understanding attitude and help in convincing his mother.

Soon after Keith and Cindy got married they moved to California where they both have good jobs as accountants in the Los Angeles area. Shortly thereafter they started attending services at the Japanese-American church in Altadena, California where we met.

When asked about their racially mixed marriage, Keith explained, "My Japanese family were active Buddhists, but I was not attending Buddhist services at the time I met Cindy. It was through the love and prayers of Cindy's mother that I became a Christian—she was so supportive of our marriage, and so loving toward me, I began to want to know more about her beliefs—and what led her to be so kind and helpful."

"Actually," added Cindy, "I wasn't a Christian either when I met Keith. My mother and sisters had been Christians for a long time, but I resisted. Then, as Keith said, Mom's loving encouragement made me more open to her Christian faith."

"I think what helped both of us finally to make a decision to become a Christian was going through the sorrow of the illness and death of Cindy's mom. We were shaken up enough to want to share her strong Christian faith," said Keith.

"Keith proved his love for me by going with me to Korean church services, even though he couldn't understand Korean." said Cindy. "That made me want to show my love for him by suggesting we go together to English services. That's how we ended up at the Altadena church."

"What are some of the minus and plus factors in your mixed marriage?" I asked.

"My mom's objections were a problem," said Keith. "And both of us have had to work hard to try to understand each other's language and culture. Also we argue a lot," added Keith. "But I think the plus factors far outweigh the minuses."

"I agree," said Cindy. "Ours is different from the usual marriage, but it is a good one. We are both well educated, share the same kind of work, and have similar values and interests—especially now that we are both Christians."

"Since you both work full time, how do you divide the home duties?" I asked.

"Well, we do have a different housework arrangement than most couples," responded Keith, "but it seems to work. For example, Cindy handles the family finances, buys my clothes and does most of the housecleaning. But I do most of the cooking."

Cindy added, "Since we both work, and I don't get home until about 8 P.M., it's a good thing Keith can cook well. He gets home earlier than I do and, of course, we eat out a lot. Sharing the workload we do get all the jobs done."

Knowing that they had been married for 13 years and had no children I asked, "How do you feel about children? Does your heavy work schedule prevent that?"

"Well," replied Keith. "For some reason we have not been able to have children. Our stressful workload might be part of the problem. We have considered adopting a child. One reason we haven't is that we know how difficult it is to take good care of children in today's dangerous world. We are not sure we could handle it well."

"Would you say that having to learn each other's language and culture is more trouble than it is worth?" I asked.

"It's well worth the effort," replied Keith. "Sharing both traditions enriches our life and our marriage. My goal is to visit Korea with Cindy soon because I'd like to know her background in Korea the same way she knows my Japanese-American life in Hawaii."

Whatever the future holds for Keith and Cindy, I believe they will handle it well. They are both quiet, dignified young people whom I have come to love and admire. They are demonstrating what it takes to make a culturally mixed marriage succeed: love, patience, coöperation, forgiveness and willingness to work out problems, plus respect for each other's culture.

12

Unraveling Ties That Bind

One day Bert appeared at my church office asking to enroll his son, Jose, in our scouting program. I was curious to note that fair-skinned Bert had a dark-skinned son. He explained, "Jose is really my adopted son. I married his Filipino mother several years ago—after she lost her Filipino husband."

After Jose started in our scouting program, the whole family started attending worship services and I met Maria, his attractive wife, who appeared some 15 years younger than Bert. After a visit to their home, I learned more about this unique family.

On one visit I noticed Jose riding around on an unusual three-wheeled cycle. When asked where Jose got that interesting cycle, Bert replied, "Oh, I'm an engineer, and I made it for him using bicycle parts. I added an extra wheel and welded it all together in that tricycle form. He uses it to deliver newspapers on his paper route. It works all right, but there is a problem. Although Jose is eleven, he is small for his age. When the cycle is heavily loaded he isn't strong enough to pedal up a hill. He has to get off and push it."

Maria added, "Sometimes I go along and help push it—until he has delivered enough papers to lighten the load enough for him to handle it alone."

Seeing Bert's efforts to help his adopted son and his obvious love for the boy were certainly admirable. To me Bert and Maria seemed to get along quite well, so I was surprised when a mutual friend said to me, "Bert says he thinks his young wife is playing around with another man."

"That's hard to believe," I replied. "Even if it is true, Bert should make sure he has adequate proof before he confronts Maria with that accusation. Who is the man Bert suspects?"

"A young student from another country," replied my friend. "Bert helped him come here to study in an American college. The foreign student spends his vacations with them—and that's when Bert thinks Maria is unfaithful—while he is at work."

Shortly thereafter I noticed that relations between Bert and Maria seemed to be getting a little cold and strained. It also seemed Bert was drinking more and more alcohol—which could be his response to increasing stress in their relationship. I not only worried about them, I began to wonder if their marriage would survive this crisis. Outwardly they continued to keep up the appearance of a successful marriage, but Bert's drinking problem gradually became worse.

One day Bert said to me, "I have applied for an engineering job with an oil company in Saudi Arabia. Life is hard there but the pay is good and I think Maria and I need a change in our life that this will provide."

Apparently, this was Bert's way of trying to solve some of their problems. He would take Maria away from the tempting dark and handsome foreign student—rather than confront her with an accusation of being disloyal.

After they left for Saudi Arabia there was not much communication from them until Maria sent some shocking news: "Bert just died of a sudden heart attack here in Saudi Arabia. The American consulate here is helping me make arrangements to ship Bert's body home for burial, but we are having problems. The Saudi government discovered Bert was having his alcohol shipped into Saudi Arabia, which is against their Muslim law. We will have to pay a big fine before they will release Bert's body. As soon as we can work out the legal problems, we will bring his body home."

This delay lasted for several weeks. When Maria and Jose finally arrived home with Bert's body, Maria was on the verge of a nervous breakdown and seemed ready to collapse from the physical, mental and spiritual strain. She wept uncontrollably at Bert's funeral and although she never confessed the details, she clearly indicated that she felt guilty about Bert's sudden death. She acknowledged that it was her unfaithfulness which made Bert drink too much, and it was his drinking that caused his heart attack—ergo her responsibility for his early death.

Maria's mental anguish was so acute, it was obvious no one need condemn her further for her unfaithfulness. She was already paying a heavy penalty of suffering for her sin—and she seemed to be repentant. Bert, who was a kind and gentle man, seemed incapable of throwing stones, let alone divorcing Maria, knowing how economically dependent she and Jose were upon him. Also, he apparently hoped by removing Maria from a possibility of temptation, she would get over her romantic interest in the young man.

This interracial marriage certainly endured with outward signs of stability. However, their relationship had been strained.

But the basic problems that weakened this mixed marriage were not racial—more likely they were those of age difference, the influence of alcohol and the effect of unfaithfulness.

And though Maria expressed regret for her unfaithfulness to Bert, after becoming a widow she fell back into a relationship with the young man who moved in with her to the home she had inherited from Bert, several weeks after the funeral. So Maria again is in an interracial relationship, but the situation is now reversed. She is at least 15 years older than the student, and, just as Maria was economically dependent upon Bert, now the young man is economically dependent upon her. Due to Bert's good economic planning, Maria was left in an enviable position. She not only inherited Bert's home, she also acquired his large savings plus a generous life insurance payment.

So only time will tell how long the young man will be content to live comfortably with a woman much older than he is. Will his pride allow him to be completely dependent upon her forever? Will he become attracted to a younger person, as happened with Maria? Surely their relationship will face struggles in the days ahead, but perhaps it will last long enough for Maria to regain some emotional stability and get on with her life.

13

A Japanese-Latino Partnership

Donna Kiriyama and Mark Gonzales met when they were both playing instruments in their high school marching band at the John Muir High School in Pasadena, California. Donna played the glockenspiel bells and Mark was a drummer.

These "bells" are tuned metal bars played with light hammers which make them sound like bells. After Mark had heard Donna skillfully playing them for quite a while, he thought, "That attractive girl, Donna, is beginning to 'ring my bell.' I'd like to get to know her better." When he learned Donna was into gymnastics he mused, "I bet she could give me a good, strong hug if she wanted to. I'll talk to her and see if she may like me."

Donna was also rather observant and, after hearing Mark's drums many times, she began thinking, "That guy is good. He really has rhythm. I bet he would make a good dance partner." One day, without realizing it, Donna began to hum the song "May I Have This Dance?"

Romantic sparks were beginning to fly in both directions, but it took nine long years, and a lot of dating, before these developed into a flame of love bright enough to consider marriage.

When Donna talked to her parents about marriage they were not sure it was a good idea. They would have preferred she marry a Japanese. But, as they got to know Mark better, they liked him and finally agreed to the marriage. Mark's folks also agreed so Donna and Mark were married in a ceremony held at our Japanese-American church in Altadena where Donna was a member and where Mark soon joined.

Although from different racial backgrounds, Donna and Mark had many things in common: they were from the same high school, went to the same college, they both liked music and were third generation American citizens. Their differences in heritage didn't matter to them.

After a year of marriage their daughter, Ambre Aki, was born, followed seven years later by the birth of their son, Daniel Taketo. The grandchildren erased any remaining objections to the marriage their respective parents held onto.

When I got to know them, I had to admire Mark, who

A Japanese-Latino Partnership

though not Japanese, put effort into taking part in church activities—an obvious demonstration of his love for Donna and his flexibility. Asked if their children identified well with both Japanese and Latino cultures, they replied, "Yes, our children are comfortable with both cultures. They have encountered a little prejudice due to their mixed racial background, but no more than other children of interracial marriages have to face."

The advantages they cited that come from such cross-cultural marriages included food: "We get to eat lots of good Japanese and Mexican food! At Christmas we always make tamales and at New Year's we make Japanese 'oshogatsu' food—such as rice dishes, teriyaki fish and chicken, besides lots of rice crackers and cookies.

"Another advantage is that our life is richer and fuller by knowing and appreciating both cultures. We hope our children will also find their lives enriched by the two languages and cultures. We are trying to pass on both these things to them."

When asked to think about the disadvantages of an interracial marriage they said, "In our case there aren't any. We both grew up with the same language and culture here in America—and see our Japanese and Latino backgrounds as extra blessings. We're glad that our parents on both sides get along well and seem to enjoy sharing their own racial heritage with us."

They also expressed satisfaction that they have many good friends from both cultures with whom they can share family celebrations and holidays. When asked what advice they would give other couples considering an interracial marriage they said, "We would tell them not to be in any hurry. Take time to get to know each other really well. And take time to think ahead regarding some of the problems that may arise. Then plan how you would try to face those challenges and overcome them.

"Think carefully about how you would handle such issues as your child rearing techniques, sharing household and family responsibilities—and any money problems you may have to face. Also consider what kind of relationships you would like to develop with family and friends. Planning ahead can avoid many hassles that could endanger your marriage. But most of all, make sure you share similar moral and religious values. Especially be careful that you agree on what moral, ethical and religious values you want to pass on to your children."

This Japanese-Latino marriage is certainly a stable role model for others. Even though they admit they have had their "ups and downs" these have not been due to their cross-cultural differences. Their problems or challenges have come more from their personality differences combined with the pressures of living in a stressful American society.

No one can accuse Donna and Mark of rushing into their cross-cultural marriage—they dated for nine years. But even though they took awhile to make up their minds, they knew what they were doing. To observers they obviously respect each other and coöperate to maintain a happy home for their two children. They and their children are active in the church and keep up with full, busy schedules. Altogether theirs is a successful interracial marriage.

14

A Rejected Korean War Bride

There were several interracial couples attending a church I once served on the East Coast. One day one of them came to me to say, "We have just met a divorced Korean War bride, Sung, who is having a hard time. Her ex-husband not only divorced her, but abandoned her with little money to survive on. She has a small apartment, but barely manages to pay her bills by working as a waitress in a restaurant and has become an angry and abrasive person. Could you visit her and see if we can help her in any way?"

I first visited with Sung one cold, winter morning—which pretty much matched her attitude. She had been hurt by Americans—and I was just another American. However, she invited me in and began to vent her wrath. As I listened sympathetically, she changed from cold withdrawal to hot anger, as she poured out her bitterness toward her ex-husband and his family. She became a small, dark bundle of nervous energy, seemingly ready to explode at any moment. Her dark eyes flashed with resentment as she told me—in halting English—

how her ex-husband's family refused to accept her and how he would hit her when he got drunk—which was often.

It soon became apparent that her anger and aggressiveness was a self-defense measure she was using to keep her sanity as she struggled to overcome the effects of the cruel treatment she had suffered. Although abrasive toward those around her, it was her assertive personality which allowed her to endure the pain of rejection—while gaining some control over her life.

After telling her a little about our church I asked her, "How did you meet the soldier whom you married in Korea?"

In broken English she replied, "I meet him in bar. My family poor. I go to city and get job—send money to family. I go only sixth grade. I no can find good job, so I work in bar. I serve drinks to soldier men. My soldier come there much. He like me. He drink many beer—too much—but I like him. One day he say, 'Let's live t'gether.' I think few days, and I say 'yes.' Long time we live in little house."

"Did he offer to marry you?" I asked.

"Not first days," replied Sung. "But when time go back America, I say, 'I wanna go America, too. Marry me.' He see Army Chapleen and talk, then we marry."

"Did the Chaplain first do some marriage counseling with you, concerning the problems you might face?" I asked.

"We go meetings," answered Sung, "but I no unnerstan English much."

"When you first came to America, did you find life hard from the very beginning?" I asked.

"Yes," answered Sung. "English hard, American ways hard. But Korea more bad for me than America. If stay in Korea I no can marry. In Korea all say, 'Bar girl is bad girl.' No man marry 'bad girl'. So I glad come to America."

"Did your husband and his family treat you badly from the beginning?" I asked.

"If no drunk my husband good, if drunk he bad—hit me!" said Sung, rapidly pumping her fist at me. His mama say, 'He drunk, your fault, go back Korea. We no want you here.'"

"Does he pay alimony to help support you?" I asked.

"Law say he pay," replied Sung. "But he no pay. He go far away. I not know his place now. His mama and papa no tell me—and they no give me money. They only say, 'Go back Korea,' 'Go back Korea.' They no good people," said Sung, spitting out the words like bad-tasting food.

"Do you want to go back to Korea?" I asked.

"Before I think maybe Korea better, now I think America better. In America I get better job. In America, someday maybe I meet good man and again marry. In Korea no man marry 'bad bar girl.' I stay here."

When I left, it was so cold my car couldn't back up the steep incline where I had parked. After several tries the motor finally warmed up enough to make it up the hill. I said a prayer of thanks and wondered if this was a sign of what was ahead with Sung. By working patiently with her, she might finally warm up to those around her and get her life moving forward here in America. As representatives of our church, maybe we who befriended her could help. I was encouraged.

After I got to know Sung better I asked, "Would you like me to give you a Bible? I think you would find many words of comfort and help from Jesus if you started reading the Bible."

"I no can read English Bible," replied Sung. "If you get Korea Bible, I read."

I contacted the nearest American Bible Society representative and asked about getting a Korean version, but they had no suggestions. Finally I decided to write directly to a missionary friend in Korea for help. Shortly I had received three copies of a bilingual New Testament with Korean on one side of the page and English on the other. I thought this might help Sung get spiritual help from the Bible as well as facilitate improving her English.

When I gave this Korean-English New Testament to Sung she seemed pleased. Awhile later, I asked, "Would you like to start coming to our church? There you could learn more about Christ and make many new friends."

"Now I no can come," replied Sung. "I work Sundee. Maybe someday I come. Now, ev'ry night I read Korea Bible, with verses you marked for me. I know God love me, and I love God and Jesus. Maybe someday I be Christian. I thank God you and Chachee (church) pray for me. You my good friends."

Soon after that we moved to the West Coast, so we entrusted her into the care of the interracial couple who first befriended her. They subsequently reported that a dynamic Korean couple became active in the church and have been reaching out—not only to Sung, but to other cross-cultural couples in need.

Sung's tragic experience is not unusual. Unfortunately many military interracial marriages have rocky histories because all too often they are based on brief liaisons that produce what turn out to be unwanted and neglected children. Having a supportive church community is a great boon to such couples who are trying to deal with cross-cultural relationships in a responsible way.

15

Expanding Horizons

When I first met Arnold and Alison, I thought they were one of the most good-looking couples I'd come across. Being from Pakistan, Arnold was tall, dark and handsome. Alison, from Scotland, was fair complected and beautiful. Their contrasts made them a strikingly attractive couple.

We met at a memorial service for Dr. Ralph Stewart, a mutual friend who had been a missionary to India and Pakistan where he had served as a teacher and principal of a Christian school, Gordon College, for 50 years. Arnold was a graduate of

Gordon and his father had been one of Dr. Stewart's students so Arnold and Alison had visited Dr. Stewart many times during his retirement before he finally died at age 103.

In talking with Arnold and Alison afterwards I realized that they were a happily married cross-cultural couple who could make a positive contribution to our interracial marriage study project. One of the motivations for this undertaking came from dealing with a couple in our church who were from completely different racial, language and cultural backgrounds and seemed to be having such trouble communicating with one another.

I was intrigued about gathering pointers from cross-cultural couples who were happy to see if we could help our struggling couple at church and thus was happy when both Arnold and Alison were willing to be involved and discuss their apparently successful interracial marriage.

Arnold and Alison met at work in London, England where both were working for a medical products laboratory. They liked each other from the beginning, but it was almost three years before they felt they were ready to get married. By this time they had transferred to do similar work with a medical products company in the U.S., but they decided their marriage ceremony should be held in England so their families could participate and they were married in a Presbyterian church near Liverpool in a typical Christian ceremony. They returned to the U.S. after visiting family and friends, loaded down with wedding presents.

When asked about the advantages of an interracial marriage, Arnold replied, "It can benefit both partners in terms of cultural enrichment. It is really up to each partner to learn to understand and appreciate the differences in their world views and learn as much as possible about the other's background."

"I have come to savor Pakistani food and clothing," added Alison. "Someday I would like to learn Arnold's difficult Urdu language, but, I must admit I'm grateful Arnold knows the English language and Western culture so well. I think that is one reason our marriage has gone so well, thus far. When he was in Pakistan Arnold came to value our Western life-style and culture from Western contacts there. Because of his excellent English skills, we have no communication barriers. But I know I should try to learn Urdu so I can better esteem Arnold's Pakistani language and culture. I hope any children we may have will be bilingual and learn about both cultures."

"Have you encountered any problems related to differences in culture?" I asked.

"Well," replied Arnold, "I do regret that Alison is unable to participate in more of the Pakistani or Indian cultural events which take place here in the Los Angeles area, but she doesn't feel ready for that yet."

Alison added, "There is one difference in our cultures that is difficult for Arnold, also. Christmas has always been a very important and enjoyable time for me. But Arnold does not enjoy the season the way I do. Maybe he is turned off by the commercialism, which has begun to dilute the spiritual meaning of Christmas. I can see beyond the commercialism to the 'reason for the season' but I can also understand why some gaudy decorations and aggressive sales pitches do bother Arnold. To some degree they bother me, too."

"What have been your happiest moments together?" I asked.

"The wedding was certainly a high point," replied Arnold. "It was a great time for us and for our family and friends—all of whom approved of our interracial marriage. We also enjoy decorating our home together. We have some differences in our tastes, but we find that our dissimilar views often complement each other—producing a richer artistic result than any one opinion would have alone."

"We also like to travel together," said Alison. "We both enjoy visiting unusual places and we hope to continue to be 'world travelers'. It is expensive, though."

"Since both of you have good jobs, I assume you don't have any serious budgetary problems," I said. "Some interracial couples I know find finances their biggest difficulty."

Arnold answered, "My life in Pakistan was an affluent one. I never had to worry about finances. Alison's background was not as prosperous as mine. Therefore, she can't seem to understand why I don't share her concern about being very careful with our spending and savings plans. In fact, it seems to me that the differences in our economic background are more of an obstacle in our marriage than those of race and culture. This is the cause of most of our arguments, anyway.

"When we do argue, Alison tries to stay calm and talk about the issues later. All our decisions, including monetary ones, are mutually agreed upon. We know this is important for the survival of our relationship. Therefore, we try hard to come to a consensus for every difference of opinion we may have. That way we are able to overcome the problems we face."

"What are the qualities you like in one another?" I asked.

Alison replied, "I not only admire Arnold's good looks, I like even more his outgoing personality and his kindness toward others. He has a deep respect for older people and is patient in dealing with them. He genuinely enjoyed visiting Dr. Stewart right up to the end of his life.

"I'm not as skilled in social relationships as Arnold is, so I get uncomfortable at some Indian events. Knowing the British exploited India and Pakistan I feel that, although Indian people are usually nice to me, they may be questioning the wisdom of our relationship. Maybe part of this is my imagination, but I do sense that some of them resent my being married to Arnold."

Regarding Alison, Arnold said, "From the first I cherished Alison's natural beauty. Now after a year of marriage, I have come to admire greatly her even temper and calmness, even when we disagree. I also like how she stays in the background, working quietly to help other people feel comfortable in her presence. A definite part of her beauty is the loveliness of her calm, kind personality."

"Arnold, before you met Alison did you ever consider going back to Pakistan to find a Pakistani bride?" I inquired.

"Not really," replied Arnold. "Too often I've observed those who have emigrated to the West from India and Pakistan going back to their native land for arranged marriages. This, in my opinion, is a sure recipe for a problematic marriage. Sometimes I've observed a few people bring back a spouse under false pretenses, pretending their social standing in the West is higher than it really is. This type of arrangement has often led to misery for the husband or wife who was brought back from the East. I think my interracial marriage to Alison is a much better one than anyone could have arranged for me in Pakistan."

It would seem this cross-cultural marriage is successful for several reasons. First, they obviously love and respect one another and work hard to overcome any problems they face. Second, Arnold's excellent English and his extended knowledge of Western culture makes it easy for them to communicate and work out the inevitable misunderstanding that arise in any relationship. Beyond this, Alison's positive attitude toward the Pakistani culture is assuring, as is her willingness to have their children raised bilingually in English and Urdu, giving Arnold the confidence she is open to his culture—even though she still has much to learn.

Referring to the cultural issue Arnold added, "At first Alison didn't realize how important my Pakistani culture is to me. She now knows I cannot suppress or deny my Pakistani views and thankfully now realizes that having two cultures to draw from can enrich our marriage. I am grateful that we don't have any major racial or cultural problems."

In addition to an appreciation of each other's culture, Arnold and Alison share similar religious ethical and moral values—an important factor in making any marriage succeed. As a graduate of a Christian mission school in Pakistan, Arnold had a lot in common with Alison who inherited a rich Presbyterian heritage from her Scottish ancestors.

Their sharing together the Christian values of love, mutual respect and forgiveness has given their marriage a firm foundation. This attractive couple has obviously been blessed by God with a healthy interracial marriage.

16

A Three-Cultures Life

My first connection with Robin and Pearl began before either of them were born. Robin's mother, Martha Asakura, introduced me to my wife, Lillian, in May 1948. She had recently returned from a Japanese internment camp and was living in a hostel put up by the Japanese Union Church in downtown Los Angeles in an area better known as Little Tokyo. At the time I was impressed with how Martha had not allowed her oppressive camp experience to make her bitter.

CROSS-CULTURAL MARRIAGES AND THE CHURCH

As part of my call to missionary service in Japan, I was serving as student pastor for the Japanese young people of Union Church. Lillian was taking lessons in Japanese from Martha, the church secretary. At the time, none of us could imagine that 46 years later I would be including her son's cross-cultural marriage story in my book. Nor could we imagine that we would be thrown together with the family because I was asked to officiate at Martha's memorial service in December 1993.

They shared their story with me. Robin relates, "Pearl and I met at Cal State University, Los Angeles where she was a sophomore and an honors student on the Dean's List. I had been working for a couple of years and was returning to continue my college education. At that time I was majoring in 'fraternity'—and I was very good at it.

"It was thanks to one of my fraternity's parties that we met. While I did not further my education, I was instrumental in destroying hers! That quarter her grades came closer to mine, a good, strong C-average. We met in January. I proposed in February. We married in May. As you can see, we don't rush into things. She has given me 18 wonderful years, two great children, and more happiness than I can ever deserve. I am looking forward to growing old with Pearl.

"Sometimes you know something is right. You might not be able to articulate why, but the confidence grows. This happened to us and it didn't take me long to decide that this is the woman I wanted to marry.

"Before our son Edmond was born we had seven marvelous years getting to know each other and building a marriage before we had to accept the responsibility of parenthood. For us, this was very helpful. When the harder times came, we were ready for them. We knew each other, and we knew what is important to us. We knew what to expect from each other."

When asked what their parents said about their marriage, Robin continued, "My parents were quite accepting of my Chinese bride. My mother was always international in her thinking and she saw the good in everyone she met. My Dad is Japanese-Hawaiian, and his sisters married a Chinese, a Filipino and a Portuguese. Race made no difference to them. My brother had already married out of the Japanese race, so my family were not bothered by my decision.

"Pearl's family had a harder time. They are first-generation Chinese-Americans and those qualities that enabled them to build lives in a culture that was foreign to them, were the traits that made it hard for them to accept the fact that their first-born was marrying outside of the Chinese race. They had to be strong-willed, steadfast in their beliefs and quite stubborn to survive and raise their family in a strange new land. To their generation these were desired traits.

"They made things difficult for us, but we also were strong-willed, steadfast and stubborn. They didn't want Pearl to see me. But it wasn't because of who I was. It was because of what I wasn't—I wasn't Chinese!

"Four weeks after I proposed to Pearl, her father forbade her to see me, ever again. This might have discouraged most young men, but fortunately I wasn't bright enough to realize what a formidable obstacle this was to our relationship.

"I talked to my parents and my brother, and then I asked Pearl to pack a suitcase. She had incredible courage, and packed that suitcase. The next day I moved her and her suitcase to my parents' home.

"That night I went to her parents' home and promised them

I would faithfully love and care for their daughter—and that we would take good care of each other. I also asked them to please take back the police report that I had 'kidnapped their daughter.'

"Their reluctant attitude continued, to some degree, even after we got married. Things don't change overnight. But, when we finally produced two grandsons for them, they were won over. And having fathered their first grandchildren—who are both *boys*—I can do no wrong, or at least nothing that cannot be forgiven.

"Both Edmond, now ten, and Derek, who is six, have brought incredible joy to our lives. They are the miracles that finally made me appear to be a worthwhile human being in Pearl's parents' eyes.

"And I guess our children's feelings about our interracial marriage have taught us a lot. Edmond is proud to tell people he is 'half Chinese, half Japanese and all American.' Derek is too young to care about such issues.

"And living in these three cultures has definite advantages. Our children enjoy the customs, holidays and other activities of all three cultures. Each January we relish the Japanese celebrations and parades and look forward to eating Japanese delicacies with Japanese friends. Then each February we participate in the Chinese New Year festival—with all its merrymaking—at Pearl's family home."

Asked what advice they would give other couples considering an interracial marriage, Peal said, "There are numerous advantages to such diverse relationship. Life can be exciting as you share cultures, histories and attitudes. Of course your children tend to derive great benefit from learning about different cultures and seeing how the two of you came together. Then as parents, it is wonderful to see how your separate cultures merge into this unique new person you've brought into the world."

She continues, "Your marriage can be strengthened because of your cross-cultural histories. I guess this depends on your attitudes toward each other and each other's culture, but in our case we have seen it as a positive force. Of course, they say that 'love knows no color and respects no boundaries'. We've proven that."

Robin adds, "I also think it's important to remember that should you encounter anyone who has a problem with your racial differences, that's their problem—not yours. With time, hopefully, those who judge you harshly may come to understand—and accept—the relationship. Time is a great teacher but in the meantime you have your own lives to get on with."

As a concerned friend of Robin's mother, I admire the way Robin and Pearl have remained committed to each other, in good times and in tough. In their situation it seemed wise for them to decide to wait awhile before taking on the responsibility of having children. This way they gave themselves room to grow together as a new couple, facing the challenges and overcoming the problems that any marriage brings.

They both feel that in the process they have learned to complement each other. Pearl has a talent in handling finances, so she takes care of that responsibility along with her other duties. Robin is more outgoing and finds it easier to be the spokesperson for the family.

Although it was a sad occasion that brought us back in contact with Martha's family, we rejoiced at meeting her son and his fine family. Robin is a worthy product of his mother who refused to be embittered by the injustice of the internment camps. Robin allowed time and loving patience to bring the healing needed with Pearl's parents.

Whenever "nicks and scrapes" occur in their three-cultures family—half-Japanese, half-Chinese and all-American—as they will in any family, Robin gives good counsel, "Usually all that is needed is a little time and a little love to heal."

Wise advice for all, it would seem. Obviously Martha's spirit lives on in the love that is shared by every member of this family.

17

The Best of Japan and America

Since Kiyoko was the best teacher in the Japanese language school in Kyoto, Japan and Bob was their best student, it was natural they should have an academic attraction to one another. Nor was it a great surprise to anyone when that began to blossom into a romantic attraction. As one student said, "Kiyoko *Sensei* (Teacher) is a beautiful Japanese woman of marriageable age. Bob is a handsome bachelor from America. It's natural that they should be attracted to one another."

"Yes," answered another student. "They spend a lot of time together in class, and that 'one-on-one' relationship encourages romantic thoughts. Since Bob had earlier training in Japanese, he doesn't fit in lower class groups, so that's why he gets to have so much private time in class with Kiyoko *Sensei*. By now, they should know one another quite well."

Neither of them are talking about exactly when or where the romantic sparks began to fly between them, but fly they did! While he was in school he had to be circumspect about any "extracurricular" deliberations, but finally after Bob graduated he decided he should do something about it and went to the head teacher of the language school to ask, "Do I have your permission to invite Kiyoko *Sensei* to a concert with me?"

"The only way I could agree to that," replied the head teacher, "is that you invite all the teachers to go. It would not look right here for an ex-student to take a teacher out alone."

Bob was not too happy about having several chaperons, or about the cost of paying for so many tickets, but he was so seriously smitten by love that he immediately agreed to the deal, "That would be fine. When shall I pick you ladies up?"

From his first missionary assignment in Tokyo, Bob began writing love letters to Kiyoko in Japanese. Being always the good teacher, Kiyoko would correct the mistakes in Bob's letters. Not even that uncomfortable experience dampened his ardor. He kept writing and arranged to see her whenever he could. Eventually he screwed up his courage and said, "Kiyoko, I love you. Will you marry me?"

Apparently there were no serious grammatical errors in his proposal, so she answered *"Hai"* (Yes). Soon thereafter they were married in a beautiful Christian wedding ceremony. Since both sets of parents agreed to the marriage, there were many relatives and friends at the wedding to share in the joy of their new life together. Of course, some of Bob's missionary colleagues were a little jealous, feeling that by marrying their best language teacher, Bob now had an unfair advantage over them.

When Bob's missionary assignment in Tokyo was completed, they both accepted a permanent missionary assignment at a promising Christian Center in Hokkaido, Japan's snowy northern prefecture. There they began a shared ministry which has continued successfully for over 40 years. The center program includes Christian meetings and conferences, classes in English, music and other subjects, weddings, worship services for deaf people and English worship services. They also have an unusual kindergarten program. By design, they choose to enroll mentally handicapped children as at least ten percent of the total enrollment. Not only that, they have developed a special support program for the parents of these handicapped children.

This ministry has required some real sacrifice on their part. Not only does the snow pile up in drifts over eight feet high in winter, but the pollution around the center and their nearby home is the "equivalent of smoking two packs of cigarettes a day" says Bob.

Over the years Kiyoko and Bob added four sons to their family, all of whom followed the cross-cultural example of their parents, keeping up the interracial marriage tradition. Ralph, the oldest son, married a lovely Afro-American doctor, and he works as a traffic controller at the busy Los Angeles airport. Larry, the youngest, married a Japanese woman and works for a company in Tokyo. Scotty and Bobby, the two middle boys, both married Caucasians and live and work in America. These products of a successful interracial marriage have replicated their parents' success.

Asked about the disadvantages of an interracial marriage, Kiyoko replies, "There is certainly a drawback in having to spend a lot of time learning each other's language and culture."

Bob adds, "And it seems as if the children tend to have some difficulty in deciding whether they want to live in Japan as a Japanese or in America as an American. Each of our boys has had to work this out in his own way—but they seem to be happy with their decisions."

The advantages of their cross-cultural marriage Kiyoko sees

includes: "Sharing in Bob's language and culture has helped to broaden my horizons. My life has been made richer and fuller through my marriage to Bob."

Bob adds, "Beyond this, sharing Kiyoko's world has certainly made my life richer and more meaningful. We enjoy the best of both worlds. The advantages of our marriage certainly far outweigh any disadvantages and having Kiyoko's help with the Japanese business matters here is a great blessing to me."

There seem to be several reasons why Kiyoko and Bob's marriage is so successful. Both are highly educated offspring of academic families—both their fathers were college professors—and so come from similar backgrounds. They are united in their dedication to Christ—and come from Christian families. They share similar values regarding the meaning of love, forgiveness and mutual support in their marriage. Both are willing to work and sacrifice to make their marriage succeed, and to make their shared ministry effective.

Both were mature adults when they first met and were old enough to know what they wanted, wise enough to wait for the right person, and smart enough to recognize the right person when they came to know one another.

Although now Kiyoko and Bob are officially "retired," it is a very active retirement. The Japanese director of the Christian Center with whom they have worked for many years is too ill with cancer to carry on his duties. On the one hand they feel they are too old for this duty—which has continued for several years—but, anxious as they are to retire, they feel obligated to provide this much-needed support for this place where they have spent so many happy years together.

18

Overcoming Intercultural Barriers

Intercultural marriages may create in some cases tensions which threaten the success of the marriage regardless of there being no apparent racial differences. Color is only skin deep, when it comes to cultural disagreements. Often what we find is that, like religion, culture is more important than race.

Rick and Maria's romance typifies the ideal, almost magical courtship which can take fire between people of different cultures. After listening to Rick's account of this classic, storybook, intercontinental romance, it is a rude awakening to hear

Maria's confession of her struggle with culture shock. Moving from the relatively quiet, peaceful life with her close-knit Portuguese community in South Africa, to the hectic, mad rush of life in Southern California disturbed Maria in ways that almost destroyed their magical marriage—endangering her health in the process.

Rick relates how their "ideal" romance and courtship developed: "You could say our marriage was 'made in Paradise' because we met at the romantic Paradise Beach on the Greek island of Myconos. I was on vacation from my job with an American company in Saudi Arabia. Maria was on holiday from her banking job in South Africa. Later I found out she had borrowed money for that 'dream vacation,' but I'm glad she did because her investment in that vacation led to our magical courtship and my marriage to this wonderful Portuguese beauty.

"I still remember the thrill when I first saw her on Paradise Beach. With my heart thumping wildly, I made my way toward this petite, olive-skinned beauty. I cautiously approached her—making a backup plan to cope with rejection. I only got to talk to my 'dream girl' about 15 minutes that first day. But I did come away with her home address: *I had Maria's address!* I was so fascinated by her, I followed her and her friend Shirley when they left Myconos for the nearby island of Paros—even though they politely refused to tell me where they were staying there. My friend, Bob, went with me due to his interest in Shirley.

"Arriving at Paros, we stood on the dock with our bags at our side. Finding housing was our first priority and it was almost time for lunch. Then a blessed event occurred. Before we could begin our search, the familiar figure of Maria's pal,

Shirley, came into view.

"I jabbed Bob's shoulder and exclaimed, 'There they are!' Maria and Shirley gracefully sauntered across our path, not more than 50 feet away. To my call of 'Maria!' the two turned toward us with surprised smiles and came to greet us. They gave us a few tips about the island and suggested some housing options, but Maria refused my request to spend the day together, saying they had some 'other plans.'

"Slightly rejected, but still hopeful, I did not give up. When the town stirred from its afternoon nap, Bob and I sat down to 'tea time' snacks at an open-air patio. We were enjoying the fabulous atmosphere and food when, you guessed it, the dynamic duo came into view again. Again they shared a few minutes with us. They backed out of our dinner invitation, but did mention they would be at an upstairs dancing bar later.

When Bob and I went to check on the dancers, the disco music was loud and appealing as we walked in, but only two were dancing on the spacious floor. As is common for Europeans, however, the two were females—Maria and Shirley. For most Americans this is a scene that needs 'fixing.' Feeling up to the task, we immediately stepped in to right the 'problem.'

"We shared probably the longest disco song in history, a coke and a little more talk that didn't make much sense through the loud music. Then it was time to call it a night as others came to dance with Maria. While true love never quite sparked in Greece, a fantastic pen-pal relationship began.

"Eight months after our Greek introduction, I headed to Johannesburg for our first true opportunity to get to know each other. Our courtship was unique because of the 2,000 miles that separated us. Her world had changed dramatically since we first met because her mom had died just a few days after she'd returned from Greece and she'd moved back home to help her father and two of her brothers who were still at home.

"During that first Johannesburg visit, Maria seemed a little uncomfortable, but as the week went on we began to enjoy each other more. Maria took off from work and lined up several sightseeing excursions for us to enjoy—and I soon found myself driving on the 'wrong' side of the road. By the time I was due to return to Saudi Arabia, I knew I was hooked and I prayed Maria was, too!

"Our letters helped and soon we were planning to get together again—this time San Francisco—at the end of a 13-state camping trip Maria had organized for herself and her brothers. Again, all went fabulously well, but the tables were turned—they met my eager family, and I was able to reciprocate with the tours and being the host.

"On my next vacation I went again to Johannesburg. Our fifth encounter was in Europe. Finally, it was the end of my Saudi career and time for our sixth meeting—and our marriage!

"We were married in Africa in a traditional Catholic wedding ceremony followed by a Portuguese-flavored reception with many Portuguese specialties to feast on. And I had to dance the infamous Portuguese 'Bird Dance', too!"

Asked about their view of international and intercultural marriages, Rick commented, "While our marriage is cross-cultural, it is not interracial and we both speak a common language which has not made communication a problem. We also know that our intercultural marriage has broadened our horizons and we feel an appreciation for other nations and their people. Our global thinking naturally expands as we occasionally get a chance to travel to Maria's home—and other countries along the way.

He added, "I was attracted to the intercultural part of our marriage. Not only was I marrying a beautiful, dark-haired 'hot-blooded' Portuguese woman, but I felt that Maria would bring her fresh, wholesome attributes to the fast-paced, materialistic Southern California world I had left three years before.

"I saw in Maria those simple values that I longed for. Her family, like most people in South Africa, aren't accustomed to the high tech 'necessities' of the U.S.—which we have become slaves to. For example, on the jet coming over Maria said she didn't want a microwave oven. Of course there was one waiting for us when we walked into our new home! Not wanting it, she still had to force herself to learn to use this present—and the pressure began.

At this point Rick began touching the intercultural problem that almost destroyed their marriage. He said, "Maria's polite and sophisticated charm was an overwhelming success in the U.S. But she became very frustrated in trying to adjust to the fast pace of life here. And I was guilty of not giving her enough opportunity to express her frustrations to me—as she faced American 'culture shock.' She was even more disconcerted when she discovered her 'holiday husband' was actually a 'work-a-holic.' Sometimes I heard her cry herself to sleep. I had not yet learned ways needed to console my bride in her struggle to adjust to the hectic, mad rush of her new life here."

When I asked Maria about this, she explained, "The culture shock was greater than I had expected. The hardest was struggling to adjust to the very different life here. For example, in South Africa stores are closed on Saturday afternoon and Sunday and people relax and enjoy life. Here most stores are open and they seemed like any other day. I longed to get back to the more relaxed life I knew in South Africa—in my own Portuguese community.

"Everything seemed stressful, even a simple trip to the supermarket, at least at first. First it would start with having to drive there on what was for me the 'wrong side' of the road—which made me nervous. Then, at the supermarket, when I asked for 'jelly' I wasted a lot of time and energy to learn that what I wanted was called 'jello' here. When I told the bag-boy who carried my groceries to my car to put them in the 'boot' he was at first puzzled and when I pointed out the 'trunk' it made him laugh at my 'funny English'—which compounded my feeling of alienation. Many 'little things' like that kept adding to my insecurity. These strains added up making me become withdrawn and depressed.

"To make matters worse, Rick, who was so relaxed when he was courting me during his vacations, turned out to be a person who was coping with a high-pressure job, with little spare time or energy to help me adjust to this new culture. I finally realized the frustration and stress were beginning to endanger my health and I was frightened for our marriage. After four months of this, I was so homesick all I wanted was to escape back to the comfort and warmth of my Portuguese family in South Africa. I was near a nervous breakdown, fearing our supposedly 'ideal' marriage would never work.

"Then, through a new friend, God came to my rescue. This dear friend had lived and worked overseas with the Campus Crusade group. Having suffered culture shock herself, she understood my frustration and patiently taught me the 'do's and don'ts' of American culture. Best of all, she led me to a deeper Christian faith and prayer life. Rick says he could see the welcome change in me. That's how God helped save my health and our marriage.

"Ironically," she adds, "I met my friend at a hated microwave class—trying to learn to use that detested oven I'd never wanted. That pesky microwave had become a symbol of my frustration with the high tech American culture—and my negative feelings were tearing me apart. Just as my friend helped me, I hope that sharing my struggle with my culture shock will help other intercultural couples with their own trials."

Rick added, "When Maria was in despair, I was in gloom. I didn't know how to help her. I knew she wanted to escape back to her comfortable South African enclave. If she had gone back, I doubt I would have had the heart to follow her and drag her back here. I, too, was facing the end of our 'ideal' marriage. But, in our desperation, God took pity upon us. Working through a dedicated Christian friend, God saved our marriage. Daily, I thank God for doing that for us."

When I asked them to share other intercultural experiences they said, "We draw strength in reflecting on our global courting and intercultural roots."

Rick added, "For myself, I like to remember my first meetings with Maria's father—neither of us being able to speak the other's language. But we could sit together at their kitchen table watching Maria prepare our evening meal. We didn't need words but our act of sharing bread at the familiar table may have eased the awkwardness of having a foreigner in the house.

"Seven years later, Maria and I returned to her home to see how her father was coping in a losing battle with cancer. We also wanted him to see his latest grandson—before his expected death from lung cancer. For a brief few days Mr. Aparicio strengthened at seeing us, delighted at meeting his new grandson, Daniel. During the last few days of our visit he became bedridden, but with his gestures and his warmth I was convinced he appreciated what I had brought to the family."

When I asked Maria what advice she would give others contemplating an intercultural marriage, she said, "One of the hardest things for me to learn to do was to share all of my problems and feelings. It requires a lot of sensitivity and love to help one another adjust to a new culture—but you need to be able to express whatever frustrations you might have regarding the new culture, new family and friends. Also it's important not to let the 'little things' pile up and become the 'last straw that broke the camel's back'. But most of all, I would say, 'Be sure to depend on God for help in your marriage'."

Reflecting on Rick and Maria's "ideal" marriage which was almost destroyed by cultural differences and misconceptions, I realized how they exemplified the strains added to a marriage by cross-cultural differences. What is normative and expected in one culture is seen as offensive, if not obnoxious, in another. In Rick and Maria's case, his work-a-holic neglect exacerbated her culture shock and feelings of alienation so that their "ideal" marriage teetered toward failure because what they valued and esteemed in life seemed so disparate. Thankfully, with God's help, they learned to address the issues that were keeping them apart. They learned that human love and God's love are different—yet both necessary for a truly meaningful marriage.

19

Conclusion

All but one of the case studies listed in this book are interracial. Most were international and intercultural as well, although four were not. One was also mixed socially, in the sense that a person of the Japanese nobility married an American "commoner." Only two were mixed religiously.

Throughout the study it has become apparent that differences in race and culture are fundamental. As the Korean wife, Sue, said, "I was greatly disappointed to find my American husband, Art, didn't like some of the Korean food I worked so hard to prepare for him. Besides, at first, I didn't know how to prepare American food."

The Pakistani husband, Arnold, was so westernized by the time they married that his Scottish wife, Alison, felt his own culture was no longer important to him. But he said, "I cannot suppress or deny my culture. I feel I must attend some Pakistani parties and cultural events, even though Alison doesn't yet feel comfortable when she goes with me."

Kenny, the American drummer married to Japanese Sumika,

said, "Sometimes I feel like I want to 'throw in the towel.' It is very hard for us to communicate because Sumika knows so little English, and is just now learning American customs. I know almost nothing about the Japanese language and culture. It is frustrating for both of us, but we are doing our best to try to understand one another. Family counseling with someone who understands both English and Japanese has helped us."

A choice insight to the problems of race and culture was made by the Filipino wife, Gloria, married to a Thai pastor: "If the ingredients of Christian love and forgiveness are in the marriage, differences in race and culture can be overcome."

Other Christian couples confirm what Gloria said and it seems that sharing common religious views and values is much more important than being from the same race or culture. As illustrated in the Biblical basis which began this study, religion is more important than race or culture.

I have encountered several marriages between Christians and Jews where the religious factor has put an extra strain on the marriage. One couple we know where a Christian woman married an Orthodox Jew encountered so much opposition from his strict Orthodox parents they held the Jewish Ceremony for the Dead for their disloyal son. For his parents he no longer existed. This couple is still together, but unless something changes their children will never know their Jewish grandparents—and vice-versa.

Not all interfaith couples face such hostility, yet often tensions over religious differences can add tremendous burdens to a relationship—especially when there are primal disagreements about whether to rear the children in one faith or the other. A not-always-satisfactory solution to religious differences is simply to ignore all religions. But this seems to avoid the problem by creating a religious void—another serious problem.

Interracial marriages between Christians and Muslims sometimes prove to be difficult. Especially when Christian women marry Muslim men they find that living under strange and stringent foreign "rules" difficult for someone raised under democracy. In some instances Western wives have described themselves as "prisoners" of their Muslim husbands. When they meet in America, the Muslim husband tends to observe Western mores, but when they return "home" and want to revert to the customs with which they grew up, they might say things such as, "Muslim law allows me to control you." Few Western women find this palatable and such marriages tend to break up—often with a lot of hostility in the process since both parties feel duped because either new rules are being instituted arbitrarily or because old rules are seen as invalid.

This is not typical of Muslim husbands who have moved to the West and married Christian wives. Usually they are happy to adopt the customs of the West and have a much better track record in working out whatever cross-cultural pressures might develop in their marriages. However whenever spouses hold strongly opposing religious views, it appears that this can cause more severe strains on a relationship than almost any other cross-cultural pressure.

It is easy to conclude that cross-cultural couples having similar religious views and values have an added foundation to their relationship that would presage a lasting success to their marriage. Most of the Christian couples interviewed for this book have been able to bring the self-giving love and the forgiving spirit of Jesus Christ into their marriage relationship. Many of these successful interracial couples have testified to the importance of having a shared world view and consonant values and see these as essential keys to the success of their marriage.

In the case studies of failed marriages given in this book none of the couples were active in the church at the time their marriage disintegrated. Surely this is not a mere coincidence. Dugan Romano lists ten "factors for success" in her book, *Intercultural Marriage* (Intercultural Press, 1988:126-127): "Good motives for the marriage. Common goals. Sensitivity to each other's needs. A liking for the other's culture. Flexibility. Solid, positive self-image. Spirit of adventure. Ability to communicate. Commitment to the relationship. And a sense of humor."

It would seem that a good addition to this list would be the importance of shared religious views and values. Everyone observing the sociology of this country is noting the increase in international and interracial marriages. Every indicator appears to evidence that they will continue to do so. Thus it would behoove us in the church to study the problems associated with such marriages so we can be helpful and supportive to these couples. And, as a related factor, we must find ways to help neglected mixed-race children, here and throughout the world.

A good place to begin is in our counseling with young people who are planning mixed marriages by helping them realize the importance of being compatible in their ethical and religious views and values. If they can incorporate the self-giving love and forgiving spirit of Jesus Christ into their relationship, their marriage will certainly be more likely to succeed.

My prayer is this book will help many cross-cultural couples and those who try to support them in meeting their challenges as they seek to build happy, rewarding lives together.

Interracial Support Organizations

Arkansas
A Place for Us
P. O Box 104
Little Rock, AR 72203
Tel: 501-888-1247

California
A Place for Us
P.O. Box 357
Gardena, CA 90248-7857
Tel: 213-779-1717

MASC (Multiracial Americans of S. Calif.)
12228 Venice Blvd. #452
Los Angeles, CA 90066
Tel: 310-836 1535

Claudia's Caravan (catalog/materials)
P. O. Box 1582
Alameda, CA 94501
Tel: 510-521-7871

I-PRIDE (Interracial Intercultural Pride)
P.O. Box 191752
San Francisco, CA 94119-1752
Tel: 415-399-9111

Assoc. of MultiEthnic Americans
P. O. Box 191726
San Francisco, CA 94119-1726
Tel: 415-548-9300

Parents' Place (workshops)
San Francisco, CA 94107
Tel: 415-563-1041

IMAGE
P.O. Box 4432
San Diego, CA 92164
Tel: 619-527-2850

Colorado
FC (Families of Color) Communique
c/o Dr. C. Lessman / P.O. Box 478
Fort Collins, CO 80522
Tel: 303-223-9658

Center for Study of Biracial Children
2300 South Krameria St.
Denver, CO 80222
Tel: 303-692-9008

District of Columbia
Interracial Family Circle
P.O. Box 53290
Washington, DC 20009
Tel: 301-229-7326

Florida
BRANCH (Biracial & Natural Children)
P.O. Box 50051
Lighthouse Point, FL 33074
Tel: 305-781-6798

Interracial Couple & Family Network
2001 Homes St.
Tallahassee, FL 32310
Tel: 904-576-6734

A Place for Us
Naples, FL Chapter
c/o Cherie Byrd
Tel: 813-732-6996

Harmony
P.O. Box 16996
West Palm Beach, FL 33416
Tel: 407-582-2182

Georgia
Interracial Family Alliance
P.O. Box 20290
Atlanta, GA 30325
Tel: 404-696-8113

Interracial Family Alliance
P.O. Box 9117
Augusta, GA 30906
Tel: 404-793-8547

Project Race / c/o Susan Graham
1425 Market Blvd. Ste 1320-E6
Roswell, GA 30076
Tel: 404-640-7100)

Illinois
Biracial Family Network
P.O. Box 489
Chicago, IL 60653-0489
Tel: 312-288-3644

Families for Interracial Awareness
Northern Chicago Area
c/o Linda Thomas
Tel: 708-869-7117

Sherry Blass, c/o Tapestry
40 Francis Ave.
Crystal Lake, IL 60014

Interracial Family Network
P.O. Box 5380
Evanston, IL 60204-5380

Child International
4121 Crestwood
Northbrook, IL 60062

Adoptive Parents Together
c/o Linda Russo
427 N. Wheaton Ave.
Wheaton, IL 60187

No. Shore Race Unity Task Force
536 Sheridan Rd.
Wilmette, IL 60091

Maine
Intercultural Press, Inc.
P. O. Box 700
Yarmouth, ME 04096
Tel: 207-896-5168

Massachusetts
Students of Mixed Heritage
Williams College / J. Kelley, SU 2303
Williamstown, MA 01267
Tel: 413-597-6141

Multiracial Family Group Network
P.O. Box 554 (Newtown Branch)
Boston, MA 02258
Tel: 617-332-6241

Michigan
Multiracial Group at U. of Michigan
K.E. Downing/122 Undergraduate Library
Ann Arbor, MI 48109-1185
Tel: 313-763-5084 or 313-764-4479

MRFY (Multi Racial Family & Youth)
P.O. Box 7521
Bloomfield Hills, MI 48302
Tel: 313-335-7629

Society for Interracial Families
P.O. Box 4942
Troy, MI 48099
Tel: 313-643-6652

Minnesota
Bridges c/o N. Bandy/Macalester College
1600 Grand Ave.
St. Paul, MN 55105
Tel: 612-699-1165

Interracial Support Organizations

Inter-Race (consultants, networking)
600 - 21st Ave. So.
Minneapolis, MN 55454
Tel: 612-339-0820

Missouri
Multiracial Family Circle
4801 Main, Box 32414
Kansas City, MO 64111

Interracial Family Unity Network
1015 Dulles St.
Jefferson City, MO 65109-2576
Tel: 314-635-6375 or 635-9899

Nebraska
Parents of Interracial Children
115 S. 46th Street
Omaha, NE 68124
Tel: 402-553-6000

New Jersey
GIFT (Getting Interracial/cultural Families Together) P.O. Box 811
Lakewood, NJ 08701
Tel: 908-364-8136 or 908-367-2755

New York
A Place for Us
P.O. Box 40-0902
Brooklyn, NY 11240
Tel: 718-622-1774

Interracial Club of Buffalo
P.O. Box 400 (Amherst Branch)
Buffalo, NY 14226
Tel: 716-875-6958

INTRace
P.O. Box 582
Forest Hills, NY 11375

North Carolina
Interracial Ministries of America
5805 Aqua Court
Charlotte, NC 28215

LIFE (Learning for Interracial Family Enrichment) P.O. Box 14123
Raleigh, NC 27620
Tel: 919-876-6574

Ohio
Cincinnati Multiracial Alliance
P.O. Box 17163
St. Bernard, OH 45217
Tel: 513-791-6023

SWIRLS Ministry
132 E. South St.
Fostoria, OH 44830
Tel: 419-435-0325

CAIFA (Cleveland Area Interracial Families) 808 East 203 Place
Euclid, OH 44119

Rainbow Families of Toledo
6146 Meadowvale Drive
Toledo, OH 43613
Tel: 419-475-3842

Multiracial Families of Central Ohio
2777 Castlewood Road
Columbus, OH 43209
Tel: 614-231-2871

Interracial Family Association
P. O. Box 34323
Parma, OH 44134
Tel: 216-348-3500

Oregon
Honor Our New Ethnic Youth
(HONEY) 454 Willamette Ave. #213
Eugene, OR 97401
Tel: 503-342-3908

Interracial Family Network
P.O. Box 12505
Portland, OR 97212

Pennsylvania
Rainbow Circle, Broadfield Association
P.O. Box 242
Chester, PA 19016

Interracial Families
5450 Friendship Ave.
Pittsburgh, PA 15232
Tel: 412-661-7414

SOME Families
1798 Unionville-Lenape Rd.
West Chester, PA 19382
Tel: 215-793-1533

Tennessee
A Place for Us
P.O. Box 11303
Memphis, TN 38111

Texas
Interracial Family & Social Alliance
P.O. Box 35109
Dallas, TX 75235-0109
Tel: 214-559-6929

Interracial Family Alliance
P.O. Box 16248
Houston, TX 77222-6248
Tel: 713-454-5018

Center for the Healing of Racism
P.O. Box 27327
Houston, TX 77225

Virginia
Interracial Connection
P.O. Box 7055
Norfolk, VA 23509
Tel: 804-622-9620

Washington
Interracial Network
P.O. Box 344
Auburn, WA 98071-0344
Tel: 206-329-5242 or 854-3756

Wisconsin
Multiracial Alliance of Wisconsin
P.O. Box 9122
Madison, WI 53715
Tel: 608-836-0616

"A Place for Us" National Chapters
Phoenix, AZ/Clyde & Susie Esprit
Tempe, AZ/Dr. Doris Jones
Fayettsville, AK/Misty Owens
Hot Springs, AR/Hercules Andrews
Little Rock, AR/Rita Frazier
Salinas, CA (N CA)/Judy Mcgee
Orange County, CA/Nadine Vazquez
Palm Springs, CA/Marty & Linda Goddard
San Diego, CA/Melvin Anderson
Bayonet Point, FL/Amy Rice
Miami Shores, FL/Patrick Dixon
Naples, FL/Cherie Byrd
W. Palm Beach, FL/John Sampson
Temperance, MI/Sheila Adkins
Minneapolis, MN/Jeani Osborne
St. Louis, MO/Carmelita Hall
Brooklyn, NY/Valerie Wilkins-Godbee
Kings Mountain, NC/Jeane Caldwell
Columbia, SC/Cinde Valle
Memphis, TN/Louis Merrill
Austin, TX/Brad & Dawn Irons
Dallas, TX/Brad & Amy Russell

Note: Check directory for telephone numbers under names listed above.

Bibliography for Further Study

Alireza, Marianne, *At the Drop of a Veil,* Boston: Houghton Mifflin, 1971.
Allen, James Paul & Eugene James Turner, *We the People: An Atlas of Ethnic Diversity,* NY: Macmillan, 1988.
Allport, Gordon W., *The Nature of Prejudice,* NY: Doubleday, 1954.
Barron, Milton, *The Blending American: Patterns of Intermarriage,* Chicago: Quadrangle Books, 1972.
Baum, Gregory & John Coleman, eds., *The Church and Racism,* NY: Seabury, 1982.
Benedict, Ruth, *Patterns of Culture,* Boston: Houghton Mifflin, 1934.
Bode, Janet, *Different Worlds,* NY: Franklin Watts, 1989.
Brogan, Dick, comp., *Not Our Kind of Folks?* Nashville: Broadman, 1978.
Bruno, Leone, *Racism,* St. Paul, MN: Greenhaven, 1986.
Condon, J.C. & Tathi Yousef, *An Introduction to Intercultural Communication,* Indianapolis, IN: Bobbs Merrill Co., 1975.
Crester, Gary A. & Joseph J. Leon, eds., "Intermarriage in the United States," *Marriage and Family Review* 5, no. 1 (1982).
Davies, Alan, *Infected Christianity,* Montreal: McGill-Queens U, 1988.
Diekman, John R., *Human Connections,* NJ: Prentice-Hall, 1982.
Dittes, James E., *Bias and the Pious,* Minneapolis: Augsburg, 1973.
Gay, Kathlyn, *The Rainbow Effect,* NY: Franklin Watts, 1987.
Golden, Marita, *Migrations of the Heart,* NY: Ballantine Books, 1983.
Gordon, Albert I., *Intermarriage—Interfaith, Interracial, Interethnic,* Boston: Beacon, 1964.
Haselden, Kyle, *The Racial Problem in Christian Perspective,* NY: Harper, 1959.
Ho, Man Keung, *Building a Successful Intermarriage between Religions, Social Classes, Ethnic Groups or Races,* St. Meinrad, IA: St. Meinrad Archabbey, 1984.
Jordon, Winthrop, *White Over Black,* Chapel Hill, NC: U of NC, 1968.
Katz, Phyllis, ed., *Towards the Elimination of Racism,* NY: Perganon, 1976.
Klimek, David, *Beneath Mate Selection and Marriage: The Unconscious Motives in Human Pairing,* NY: Van Norstrand Reinhold, 1979.
Kochman, Thomas, *Black and White Styles in Conflict* Chicago: U of Chicago Press, 1981.
Kohls, L. Robert, *Survival Kit for Overseas Living,* Yarmouth, ME: Intercultural Press, 1984.
Kurian, G., ed., *Cross-Cultural Perspectives of Mate Selection and Marriage,* Westport, CT: Greenwood Press, 1979.
Larsson, Clotye, ed., *Marriage Across the Color Line,* Chicago: Johnson, 1965.
Lederer, William J., *Marital Choices,* NY: W. W. Norton & Co., 1981.

Lee, Daniel B., *Military Transcultural Marriage: A Study of Marital Adjustment between American Husbands and Korean-born Spouses,* Salt Lake City: U of Utah, Graduate School of Social Work, nd.

Mace, D.R. & V. Mace, *Marriage East and West,* Garden City, NY: Doubleday, 1960.

Mahmoody, Betty, with William Hoffer, *Not Without My Daughter,* NY: St. Martin's Press, 1983.

Miln, Louise Jordan, *Mr. & Mrs. Sen,* NY: Frederick A. Stokes, 1923.

Montague, Ashley, *Man's Most Dangerous Myth: The Fallacy of Race,* NY: Oxford University Press, 1974.

Osseo-Asare, Francislee, *A New Land to Live In,* Downers Grove, IL: Inter Varsity, 1977.

Pannell, William E., *My Friend the Enemy,* Waco, TX: Word, 1968.

Pascoe, Elaine, *Racial Prejudice,* NY: Franklin Watts, 1985.

Perkins, John, *With Justice for All,* Ventura, CA: Gospel Light, 1982.

Prinzing, Fred & Anita, *Mixed Messages: Interracial Marriage,* Chicago: Moody, 1991.

Roman, Dugan, *Intercultural Marriage: Promises and Pitfalls,* Yarmouth, ME: Intercultural Press, 1988.

Salley, Columbus & Ronald Behm, *What Color Is Your God?* Secaucus, NJ: Citadel, 1988.

Sawdey, Michael, ed., *Women in Shadows: Military Wives,* La Jolla, CA: National Committee Concerned with Asian Wives of U.S. Servicemen, 1981.

Shackford, Kate, ed., "Children of Interracial Families," *Interracial Books for Children Bulletin* 15, no. 6:4-15.

Spickard, Paul R., *Mixed Blood,* Madison, WI: U of Wisconsin Press, 1989.

Stuart, Irving R. & Lawrence E. Abt, eds., *Interracial Marriage: Expectations and Realities,* NY: Grossman, 1973.

Tannen, Deborah, *That's Not What I Meant,* NY: Ballantine Books, 1986.

Tseng, W.S., J.F. McDermott & T.W. Maretzki, *Adjustment in Intercultural Marriage,* Honolulu: University of Hawaii Press, 1977.

Washington, J.R., Jr., *Marriage in Black and White,* Boston: Beacon, 1971.

Werkman, Sidney, *Bringing Up Children Overseas,* NY: Basic Books, 1977.

White, Steve & Ruth, *Free Indeed: The Autobiography of an Interracial Couple,* Gardena, CA: A Place for Us, 1989.

Williamson, Joel, *New People: Miscegenation and Mulattoes in the United States,* NY: New York University, 1980.

Wolfgang, Aaron, ed., *Nonverbal Behavior, Perspectives, Applications, Intercultural Insights,* Lewiston, NY: Hogrefe, 1984.

Born in Virginia, Dr. J. Lawrence Driskill and his family served as missionaries to Japan for over two decades. A graduate of Penn State University, Princeton Seminary and San Francisco Theological Seminary, he wrote his doctoral dissertation on a study of evangelism in Japan's Senri Newtown—a huge housing complex for 150,000 new residents. After leaving Japan, Dr. Driskill has served churches in Texas, Tennessee and California. Presently he lives in Duarte, California and continues to assist Japanese-American congregations in the Los Angeles area, preaching in both English and Japanese.

Additional copies of this book may be obtained
from your local bookstore,
or by sending $11.95 per paperback copy, postpaid,
or $19.95 per library hardcover copy, postpaid,
to:

Hope Publishing House
P.O. Box 60008
Pasadena, CA 91116

CA residents please add 8¼% sales tax
FAX orders to: (818) 792-2121
Telephone VISA/MC orders to (800) 326-2671